Jackson College Library
WITHDRAWN

GETTING HOOKED
Fiction's Opening Sentences 1950s-1990s

edited by Sharon Rendell-Smock

GETTING HOOKED
Fiction's Opening Sentences 1950s-1990s

edited by Sharon Rendell-Smock

© Copyright 1996 Sharon Rendell-Smock

All rights reserved; no part of this publication may be reproduced, stored in a retrieval system, or transmitted, in any form or by any means, electronic, mechanical, photocopying, recording, or otherwise, without the prior written permission of the author.

Manufactured in the United States of America
I.S.B.N. 0-9654981-0-7

For Paul

Contents

Introduction	i
Our Life in the 1950s	1
Mystery	3
Pseudonym Quiz: Mystery Authors	6
Science Fiction	7
Pseudonym Quiz: Collaborative Teams	9
Pseudonym Quiz:	
Mystery and Western Authors	10
Mainstream	11
Banned Books	14
Western	16
Romance	18
Our Life in the 1960s	20
Mystery	22
Science Fiction	25
Mainstream	28
Western	31
Romance	33
Our Life in the 1970s	35
Mystery	37
Science Fiction	39
Pseudonym Quiz: Science Fiction Authors	41
Mainstream	42
Pseudonym Quiz: Mainstream Authors	44
Western	45
Romance	47
Our Life in the 1980s	49
Mystery	51
Mystery Authors' Trademarks	53

Science Fiction	54
Mainstream	56
Western	59
Romance	61
Pseudonym Quiz: Romance Authors	63
Our Life in the 1990s	64
Mystery	66
Science Fiction	68
Science Fiction Mysteries	70
Mainstream	71
Western	74
Romance	76
Who Said That? Game	78
Answers to Who Said That? Game	87
Answers to page 6's Pseudonym Quiz: Mystery Authors	87
Answers to page 9's Pseudonym Quiz: Collaborative Teams	87
Answers to page 10's Pseudonym Quiz: Mystery and Western Authors	88
Answers to page 41's Pseudonym Quiz: Science Fiction Authors	88
Answers to page 44's Pseudonym Quiz: Mainstream Authors	88
Answers to page 63s Pseudonym Quiz: Romance Authors	88
About the Editor	89

Introduction

This volume covers the last fifty years of writing. As Tofler predicted in *Future Shock*, the accelerating pace of technological advancements in the last half of the twentieth century has challenged our ability to absorb and process these events.

If Thomas Edison could see us now! I wish I could take him by the hand and lead him to discover all we've created since that great inventor died in 1931.

Just think of what anyone born in 1930 has seen in his sixty-some years before retirement. He may have lost relatives in World War II. As he grew up his family finally got indoor plumbing. His party-line telephone went to a private one. A lot of homes in the U.S. were buying color televisions. Before long, those TVs got remote control channel-changers, then VCRs so at any time of the day or night they could watch their taped shows—and fast-forward all the commercials.

Sometime later that person got a touch tone, trim-line phone, then a machine to answer it, a FAX machine, books on tape, CDs and a player, a personal computer--maybe lap-top--desktop publishing, and Internet communication. His new car options included air conditioning, cruise control, cellular telephone, and a stereo radio/tape player/CD player.

In the medical field, breakthroughs included organ transplants and artificial limbs.

And this list represents only a fraction of discoveries since 1930.

Some men walked on the moon. Several leaders were assassinated. That's a lot to assimilate, as Tofler said.

Events of a given era shaped writers' work. I have compiled a sampling of books written in the last fifty years—in and after wartime and while history and world records were being written.

I introduce each decade with a summary of what our world was like at that time in terms of technological advances, natural catastrophes, political leanings, cultural trends and popular entertainment.

I follow this historical information with the opening sentences of that decade's fiction. I chose entries from both obscure and popular authors, from best-sellers, genre recommended reading, and Hugo, Nebula, Edgar, and Pulitzer winners.

You'll be surprised by some sentences I included—that is, until you read the sources cited. A few famous novels open with mediocre sentences. Yet the authors went on to produce stories we couldn't put down.

Boxed sidebars throughout the book set off famous quotations, pseudonym games, trends, and other interesting info (such as a list of banned books that overcame this designation and became classics).

The trivia game **Who Said That?** is the final section of *Getting Hooked*.

All fiction basically follows one blueprint: setting, plot, tension between characters, and resolution. Often a novel has more than one story line.

And of course, details of place and time period must be true to life. A passage referring to the legalized gambling in Washington, D.C., unless set in the time frame of the future, would destroy an author's credibility.

Beyond fiction's shared aspects, mystery, science fiction, western, and romance each has its own genre-specific story pattern.

Mystery: This genre may take place in any time period and setting. Heroes/heroines hold a variety of occupations, such as investigator, detective, police officer, coroner, psychologist, salvage consultant, retired bookkeeper, attorney, bank officer. The plot may involve staking out, tailing, blackmailing, kidnapping, and murdering by many methods. Realism is crucial to these suspense/thriller tales.

The hard-boiled detective of the 40s and 50s got his start in the dime novels and pulp magazines of 1910-1930, such as *Black Mask*, *Dime Detective*, *Clues*, and *Detective Story*. The hard-boiled detective's style was fast-talking, fast-shooting, cocky.

In one novel the writer may incorporate story lines covering the psychological makeup of criminals, corruption, the environment, and pollution. Some, like Carl Hiaasen, use social satire to drive home the point.

Many mystery writers portray their concern about our environment. However, this isn't the only ecology-minded genre. Mystery and science fiction share many such themes.

Science fiction: Common settings are galaxies, parallel universes, robots, androids, and aliens. Themes often involve utopia, colonization of other worlds, time travel (in the near or far future), paranoia, invisibility, evolution, overpopulation, and immortality (including cryonic preservation).

Often science fiction has its own terminology. However, the stories must be based on fact, such as the known distances between planets.

Examples of science fiction writers mastering satire and irony are Michael Moorcock, Kurt Vonnegut, Jr., and Evelyn Waugh.

Western: Set in the Old West, characters include trappers, cowboys, mountaineers, and Indians. Westerns thrive on conflicts between men and those between man and nature. Again, time frame must be accurate: Aficionados will know when a Jennings repeating rifle was invented.

Romance: The historical time period must be realistic, often contemporary or gothic. Common settings are war, plantations, the south. The plot often portrays the heroine married to a man with a secret, or as an orphan involved with the man of the house. Plots may involve graphic action, violence, and passion (and fainting). Some authors combine romance and mystery.

This book is intended for both fun and serious contemplation.

Fun: Get warm fuzzies remembering your favorite authors' work.
Sometimes you'll chuckle at a book's title.

Learn: Extrapolate, discover, and analyze authors' techniques.

View these authors' openers as a preview of their work. If you are intrigued by the first sentence you may want to read that particular book, perhaps not for the first time.

Our Life in the 1950s

Events:

* President Truman signed Japanese peace treaty.
* 1952-1961 Eisenhower was our 34th president.
* The 49th and 50th states were added to the union: Alaska ('58) and Hawaii ('59).
* The U.S. tested hydrogen bombs.
* U.S. had the world's first atomic submarines.
* Albert Schweitzer was awarded the Nobel peace prize.
* Salk established the polio vaccine.
* Billy Graham began his career as evangelist.
* Albert Einstein passed away.
* Joseph Stalin died of a stroke.
* In 1959 Castro took over Cuba.

Entertainment:

* By the mid 50s, Elvis Presley had made singing history, while Marilyn Monroe became the big screen's sex symbol.
* Soap operas moved from radio to TV.
* Amos 'n Andy Show on TV 1951-1953.
* In the first I Love Lucy show in 1951, Lucille Ball began her long comedy career.

Films:

* Rear Window
* Rio Bravo
* The King and I
* West Side Story
* Bridge on the River Kwai
* The Sound of Music
* The Pride and the Passion
* The African Queen
* Singin' in the Rain

Culture:

* Frank Lloyd Wright
* Salvadore Dali
* Robert Frost
* My Fair Lady on Broadway
* Pablo Picasso
* Big Bang theory of creation
* Margaret Mead's *Social Anthropology*
* B.F. Skinner's *Science and Human Behavior*

Notable:

* Prince of Monaco married Grace Kelly.
* Diners' Club Inc. issued the first credit card.
* First human kidney transplant performed.
* The American Medical Association documented lung cancer's association with smoking.
* Baby boom underway (1946-1964)
* Air conditioning became available in cars.
* Technology: First clock radio (dial, not digital), and first color television. First computer created that could add two 24-digit numbers in a fraction of a second.

Mystery

He hurried out of the lighted foyer of the church into the cool night, hoping that the girl with the insolent red mouth had waited for him.
Wade Miller, *Devil May Care*, 1950

The first time I saw the publisher's daughter she wore slippers and a couple of scant strips of black cloth and a cigarette.
Bruno Fischer, *The Lady Kills*, 1951

All I had to do to earn some dough was kill a guy.
Bruno Fischer, *The Fast Buck*, 1952

Most people won't even open the door when someone rings their bell.
Harold Q. Masur, *So Rich, So Lovely and So Dead*, 1952

Like everybody else, he wanted a handout.
Bruno Fischer, *Run for Your Life*, 1953

That last stretch of forty-odd miles was the worst of the entire trip.
Howard Browne, *Thin Air*, 1953

The first time I laid eyes on Terry Lennox he was drunk in a Rolls-Royce Silver Wraith outside the terrace of The Dancers.
Raymond Chandler, *The Long Goodbye*, 1953

The man at the safe worked swiftly but without haste.
John Creasey, *The Baron in France*, 1953

I met the boy on the morning of the kidnapping.
Ross Macdonald, *Meet Me at the Morgue*, 1953

The young man in the hospital bed threw out an arm and turned over.
Patricia Wentworth, *The Ivory Dagger*, 1953

He ran after the twin taillights as a car finally swerved to the side of the highway in response to his thumb signal.
Donald Hamilton, *Night Walker*, 1954

A peculiar ritual took place every evening when Wilma Rathjen came home from work.
Helen Nielsen, *The Woman on the Roof*, 1954

He had been on the job only a week but he had got used to sitting in a dead man's chair.
Dale Wilmer, *Dead Fall*, 1954

It never pays to resist arrest.
Harold Q. Masur, *Tall, Dark and Deadly*, 1956

It came by regular mail in a cheap white envelope that could have been purchased at any dime store.
Helen Nielsen, *Seven Days Before Dying*, 1956

The dove-colored Chevrolet was parked fifty feet from the hospital entrance.
Ellery Queen, *Inspector Queen's Own Case*, 1956

Most of the people who come to see Nero Wolfe by appointment, especially from as far away as Nebraska, show some sign of being in trouble, but that one didn't.
Rex Stout, *Might as Well Be Dead*, 1956

Mrs. McGillicuddy panted along the platform in the wake of the porter carrying her suitcase.
Agatha Christie, *What Mrs. McGillicuddy Saw*, 1957

The first time I saw her she was in trouble.
Bruno Fischer, *Murder in the Raw*, 1957

The parole officer came to the house on a hot Saturday afternoon in October.
John D. MacDonald, *The Price of Murder*, 1957

Something unpleasant was going to happen, something incredibly and overwhelmingly unpleasant.
Craig Rice, *Knocked for a Loop*, 1957

The voice on the telephone seemed to be sharp and peremptory, but I didn't hear too well what it said—partly because I was only half awake and partly because I was holding the receiver upside down.
Raymond Chandler, *Playback*, 1958

From the verandah where she had been left to wait she could see the golf course adjoining the hospital grounds.
Kenneth Millar, *The Three Roads*, 1958

There was something wrong with the swans that May afternoon.
Nicholas Blake, *The Widow's Cruise*, 1959

The eyes behind the wide black rubber goggles were cold as flint.
Ian Fleming, *From a View to a Kill*, 1959

It was Jobbo first told me about the car snatches.
Ed McBain, *Big Man*, 1959

From the broom closet, Consuela could hear the two American ladies arguing in Room 404.
Margaret Millar, *The Listening Walls*, 1959

You could always blame it on the heat...
Wade Miller, *Kitten with a Whip*, 1959

Where the Sleuths Live

Mystery authors writing a series often place their characters (detectives, homicide investigators, salvage consultant, coroner, and so on) on the perimeters of our continent. Sleuths are concentrated in Boston, New York, Virginia, Florida, Louisiana, California, and Washington.

Cats in the Pages

Cats live in the pages of these women mystery writers:
Linda Barnes, Christianna Brand, Lilian Braun,
Carole Nelson Douglas, Sue Grafton,
Patricia Highsmith, Patricia Moyes, Dell Shannon,
Mary Stewart, and Pauline Glen Winslow.

Pseudonym Quiz: Mystery Authors

Match these pen names with their authors. Some of them write under more than one pseudonym, as well as their own names. Answers are on page 87.

Pseudonym

1. A.A. Fair
2. Josephine Tey
3. David Frome
4. Hugh Pentecost
5. Ed McBain
6. Oliver Bleeck
7. George Orwell
8. John LeCarre
9. Barbara Vine
10. Carr or Carter Dickson
11. Ross Macdonald
12. Dell Shannon; Lesley Egan
13. Patricia Wentworth
14. Thomas Costain
15. Leslie Charteris
16. William Haggard
17. Edgar Box
18. Sara Woods
19. Michael Collins
20. Brett Halliday
21. Catherine Aird
22. Tucker Coe; Richard Stark
23. Mickey Spillane
24. William Arden
25. Charles L. Leonard
26. Amanda Cross

Author Name

a. Erle Stanley Gardner
b. Donald Westlake
c. Gore Vidal
d. Judson Philips
e. John Dickson Carr
f. Dennis Lynds
g. Pat Hand
h. Evan Hunter
i. Kinn Hamilton McIntosh
j. Eric Blair
k. Elizabeth MacKintosh
l. Mrs. Zenith Jones Brown
m. Ruth Rendell
n. David Dresser
o. Frank Morrison Spillane
p. Ross Thomas
q. Leslie Charles Bowyer Yin
r. Richard Clayton
s. David John Moore Cornwell
t. Elizabeth Linington
u. Sara Hutton Bowen-Judd
v. Dora Amy Dillon Turnbull
w. Kenneth Millar
x. Mary Violet Heberden
y. Dora Amy Elles
z. Carolyn Gold Heilbrun

Science Fiction

Brother Jarles, priest of the First and Outermost Circle, novice in the Hierarchy, swallowed hard against his churning anger; bent every effort to make his face a mask—not only to the commoners, for that was something every member of the Hierarchy was taught to do, but to his brother priests as well.
Fritz Leiber, *Gather, Darkness!*, 1950

It was a pleasure to burn.
Ray Bradbury, *Fahrenheit 451*, 1951

"So this is the first time you've been upstairs?" said the pilot, leaning back idly in his seat so that it rocked to and fro in the gimbals.
Arthur C. Clarke, *The Sands of Mars*, 1951

The soft purr of the turbine was almost lost in the roar of wind as the gray sedan traveled south through the New Mexico night.
John D. MacDonald, *Wine of the Dreamers*, 1951

The world, Branson thought, is like that circus act of long ago, back in the sweet-colored days of childhood, when the big top was as high as the sky, and gigantic horses marched the earth.
John D. MacDonald, *Ballroom of the Skies*, 1952

The idiot lived in a black and gray world, punctuated by the white lightning of hunger and flickering of fear.
Theodore Sturgeon, *More Than Human*, 1952

The Secretary-General of the United Nations stood motionless before the great window, staring down at the crawling traffic on Forty-Third Street.
Arthur C. Clarke, *Childhood's End*, 1953

The trap had closed at sundown.
Poul Anderson, *Brain Wave*, 1954

The bars are geneo in lattimer in 1963.
Edgar Pangborn, *A Mirror for Observers*, 1954

The place was cheap and dirty and smelled bad, just about the scurviest-looking dive Jeff Meyer had ever seen in his twenty-one years, and he had seen plenty of them lately.
Alan E. Nourse, *The Mercy Men*, 1955

There are very good reasons for everything they do.
Eric Frank Russell, *Men, Martians, and Machines*, 1955

As John Amalfi emerged on to the narrow, worn granite ledge with its gritty balustrade, his memory encountered one of those brief boggles over the meaning of a word which had once annoyed him constantly, like a bubble in an otherwise smoothly blown French horn solo.
James Blish, *Earthman, Come Home*, 1956

At seven A.M., Allen Purcell, the forward-looking young president of the newest and most creative of the Research Agencies, lost a bedroom.
Philip K. Dick, *The Man Who Japed*, 1956

Bordman walked that morning when the partly-opened port of his sleeping-cabin closed of itself and the room-warmer began to whir.
Murray Leinster, *The Planet Explorer*, 1956

Pippin looked out from the shelter of Gandalf's cloak.
J.R.R. Tolkien, *The Return of the King*, 1956

Stubbornly Elijah Bailey fought panic.
Isaac Asimov, *The Naked Sun*, 1957

It was a quiet morning, the town covered over the darkness and at ease in bed.
Ray Bradbury, *Dandelion Wine*, 1957

"Lot ninety-seven," the auctioneer announced. "A boy."
Robert A. Heinlein, *Citizen of the Galaxy*, 1957

Macrae had taken twenty-four photographs the previous night.
Charles Eric Maine, *The Isotope Man*, 1957

That morning, James Harker was not expecting anything unusual to happen.
Robert Silverberg, *Recalled to Life*, 1957

For a moment Kerrel Stevens was half conscious again.
A.J. Merak, *Hydrosphere*, 1959

Helen Ranston smiled sadly to herself, while she sat waiting for her husband to die.
Rog Phillips, *The Involuntary Immortals*, 1959

Everyone now knows how to find the meaning of life within himself.
Kurt Vonnegut, *The Sirens of Titan*, 1959

Pseudonym Quiz: Collaborative Teams

The authors listed below collaborate to write mystery or science fiction under pseudonyms. Can you match the writing teams and pen names? Answers are on page 87.

Pseudonym   **Authors**

1. Emma Lathen   a. Bob Wade & Bill Miller
2. Wade Miller   b. Frederic Dannay & Manfred B. Lee
3. Robert Randall   c. Cyril M. Kornbluth & Frederik Pohl
4. Ellery Queen   d. Cyril Henry Coles & Adelaide Manning
5. Peter Antony   e. Robert Silverberg & Randall Garrett
6. S.D. Gottesman   f. Audrey Kelley & William Roos
7. Manning Coles   g. Mary J. Latis & Martha Hennissart
8. Paul Dennis Lavond   h. Peter & Anthony Shaffer
9. Scott Mariner   i. Cyril Kornbluth, Frederik Pohl, &
10. Kelley Roos   Robert Lowndes

Some pseudonyms have pseudonyms!

George Sanders and Gypsy Rose Lee were pen names of Craig Rice, whose name was Georgiana Ann Randolph [who happened to be Mrs. Laurence Lipton].

Floating or house names, are often used to hide the fact that one author contributed several articles for a given magazine issue. Two house names are Ivar Jorgensen, Brett Sterling.

Pseudonym Quiz: Mystery & Western Authors

More pen names to match with their authors. Some of them write under more than one pseudonym. Answers are on page 88.

Pseudonym

1. Anthony Morton
2. Evan Hunter
3. Fritz Leiber
4. David Axton
5. K.R. Dwyer
6. John Loxmith
7. Matilda Hughes
8. Robert Caine Frazer
9. Tex Burns
10. Dr. A
11. Kyle Hunt
12. Paul French
13. Richard Marsten
14. Ed McBain
15. James Marsden
16. Brian Coffey
17. Trevor Staines
18. Hunt Collins
19. Keith Woodcott
20. Ezra Hannon
21. J.J. Marric
22. Alisa Craig
23. Philip Latham
24. Jack Foxx
25. Leslie Ford
26. Alex Saxon

Author Name

a. Louis L'Amour
b. Isaac Asimov
c. Dean R. Koontz
d. Charlotte Macleod
e. Salvatore Lombino
f. John Brunner
g. Francis Lathrop
h. Robert S. Richardson
i. John Creasey
j. Bill Pronzini
k. Leslie Ford

Mainstream

I am always drawn back to places where I have lived, the houses and their neighborhoods.
Truman Capote, *Breakfast at Tiffany's*, 1950

On Wednesday evenings Paul's mother took the tram from her work in the City Hall to the mid-week service at Merrion chapel and he usually walked over from the university, after his five o'clock philosophy class, to meet her as she came out.
A.J. Cronin, *Beyond This Place*, 1950

When he finished packing, he walked out on to the third-floor porch of the barracks brushing the dust from his hands, a very neat and deceptively slim young man in the summer khakis that were still early morning fresh.
James Jones, *From Here to Eternity*, 1951

If you really want to hear about it, the first thing you'll probably want to know is where I was born, and what my lousy childhood was like, and how my parents were occupied and all before they had me, and all that David Copperfield kind of crap, but I don't feel like going into it, if you want to know the truth.
J.D. Salinger, *Catcher in the Rye*, 1951

He was of medium height, somewhat chubby, and good looking with curly red hair and an innocent gay face, more remarkable for a humorous air about the eyes and large mouth than for any strength of chin or nobility of nose.
Harmon Wouk, *The Caine Mutiny*, 1951

Everyone had always said that John would be a preacher when he grew up, just like his father.
James Baldwin, *Go Tell it On the Mountain*, 1952

He was an old man who fished alone in a skiff in the Gulf Stream and he had gone eighty-four days now without taking a fish.
Ernest Hemingway, *The Old Man and the Sea*, 1952

I first met him in Piraeus.
Nikos Kazantzakis, *Zorba the Greek*, 1952

The Salinas Valley is in northern California.
John Steinbeck, *East of Eden*, 1952

The desk at the Grand Hotel in Bombay was crowded with incoming guests.
Pearl S. Buck, *Come My Beloved*, 1953

Herr Joseph Giebenrath, jobber and middleman, possessed no laudable or peculiar traits distinguishing him from his fellow townsmen.
Hermann Hesse, *Beneath the Wheel*, 1953

St. Botolphs was an old place, an old river town.
John Cheever, *The Wapshot Chronicle*, 1954

The boy with fair hair lowered himself down the last few feet of rock and began to pick his way toward the lagoon.
William Golding, *Lord of the Flies*, 1954

It was love at first sight.
Joseph Heller, *Catch-22*, 1955

The great curving stairway hung delicately between the floors like an unsupported cloud as though designed only for light, happy, unladen feet; but the two men, with no thought of the beauty of its architecture, descended it now heavily and without speaking.
Agnes Sligh Turnbull, *The Golden Journey*, 1955

By the time they had lived seven years in the little house on Greentree Avenue in Westport, Connecticut, they both detested it.
Sloan Wilson, *The Man in the Gray Flannel Suit*, 1955

Customs of courtship vary greatly in different times and places, but the way the thing happens to be done here and now always seems the only natural way to do it.
Herman Wouk, *Marjorie Morningstar*, 1955

May I, monsieur, offer my services without running the risk of intruding?
Albert Camus, *The Fall*, 1956

Life was sometimes puzzling to Lavinnia Winslow, but it was never dull and she could remember when it had begun to seem both bewildering and more exciting.
Frances Parkinson Keyes, *Blue Camellia*, 1957

The younger living room would be a comfortable and well-ordered room if it were not for a number of indestructible contradictions to this state of being.
Lorraine Hansberry, *A Raisin in the Sun*, 1958

On they went singing Rest Eternal, and whenever they stopped, their feet, the horses, and the gusts of wind seemed to carry on their singing.
Boris Pasternak, *Dr. Zhivago*, 1958

John Pascoe must have created something like a record for a pilot in civil aviation, because he went on flying a D.C.6b across the Pacific from Sydney to Vancouver as a senior captain of AusCan Airways till he was 60 years old.
Nevil Shute, *The Rainbow and the Rose*, 1958

The airplane plip-plopped down the runway to a halt by the big sign: WELCOME TO CYPRUS.
Leon Uris, *Exodus*, 1958

Few born serfs, like me, could tell you their birthdate, but I was born in that memorable year of 1881 when the peasants, armed only with the tools of their trade, supported by a few soldiers back from the wars, and a few priests with hearts of compassion rose up against their masters, against the laws and the customs that made a serf the property of his lord.
Norah Lofts, *The Townhouse*, 1959

Millions upon millions of years ago, when the continents were already formed and the principal features of the earth had been decided,
there existed, then as now, one aspect of the world that dwarfed all others.
James A. Michener, *Hawaii*, 1959

There is no substitute for talent.
Aldous Huxley, Point Counter Point, 1928

Banned Books

At some time in the past, these books were banned, usually by school systems:

The Adventures of Sherlock Holmes
The Adventures of Tom Sawyer and Huckleberry Finn
Alice's Adventures in Wonderland
The American Heritage Dictionary
Ancient Evenings
Candide
Canterbury Tales
Catch-22
Catcher in the Rye
Citizen Tom Paine
The Clan of the Cave Bear
The Color Purple
Deliverance
The Diary of Anne Frank
Doctor Zhivago
East of Eden
Fanny Hill
A Farewell to Arms
For Whom the Bell Tolls
Forever Amber
From Here to Eternity
The Godfather
The Grapes of Wrath
The Great Gatsby
Hamlet
Hansel and Gretel

Banned Books (continued)

I, Claudius
King Lear
Lady Chatterley's Lover
Leaves of Grass
Little Red Riding Hood
Madame Bovary
Merchant of Venice
Nineteen Eighty-Four
One Flew Over the Cuckoo's Nest
The Prince of Tides
Robin Hood
The Scarlett Letter
Sherlock Holmes
Silas Mariner
Slaughterhouse-Five
Sophie's Choice
Ulysses
Where's Waldo?

The greatest part of a writer's time is spent in reading, in order to write; a man will turn over half a library to make one book.

Samuel Johnson, in Boswell's *Life*, 1775

Western

Gospel Cummings raised his head slightly with an inquiring expression in his narrowed brown eyes.
Chuck Martin, *The Lobo Breed*, 1950

Right now, Clay Ballard was sorry he had picked up the middle-aged couple with their stalled covered wagon and delicate young blonde who had paid to ride out with them.
Bob Jasper, *Feud at Sundown*, 1951

Hopalong Cassidy stalked his white gelding on the bald backbone of the ridge.
Louis L'Amour, *The Trail to Seven Pines*, 1951

When a blizzard sweeps across the range, snow is an enemy of man and beast.
Lee Floren, *Rifles on the Rimrock*, 1952

It was crowding four o'clock of as hot an afternoon as the San Simon country had endured in forty summers when the boss of the outfit—still with that crusty look on his cheeks—climbed into the saddle and kneed his gaunt buckskin up the clatterous slope.
Nelson Nye, *Desert of the Damned*, 1952

He rolled the cigarette in his lips, liking the taste of the tobacco, squinting his eyes against the sun glare.
Louis L'Amour, *Hondo*, 1953

Rain fell from the gray spring sky, cold, dreary, endless.
Bill Gulick, *A Thousand for the Cariboo*, 1954

I do not like my father, Bartram Nathan.
Wayne D. Overholser, *The Violent Land*, 1954

During a lifetime a man may hear many varied sounds that, at a distance, resemble momentarily those made by gunfire.
William Colt MacDonald, *Destination Danger*, 1955

The tough little trail town of Sulphur Springs was no more than a wide space on the Jones and Plummer Trail out of Texas.
Lloyd Madison, *Bullet Breed*, 1955

Neale stared through the shutters of the bar at the empty street in the yellow sunlight, the Mercury sedan and the hurrying man in the brown shirt and trousers; and he was caught in a quick suspense before decision.
Michael Barrett, *The Reward*, 1956

Kate Barrow saw the rider swing into view at the far end of Jackson Street, and even though it was night she recognized the bulk of the man against the low-hanging stars.
Barry Cord, *The Guns of Hammer*, 1956

Indecent, that's what the day had been, each hour smoking its way past as if spewed from hell, directly at Texas, with warmest regards.
Al Dewlen, *The Night of the Tiger*, 1956

It was late spring along the river.
Dean Owen, *The Gunpointer*, 1956

He had stopped last night in the Gunsight Hills making dry camp because others had reached the water hole before him and he preferred to avoid other travelers.
Louis L'Amour, *Last Stand at Popago Wells*, 1957

The mules strained forward strongly, hoofs stomping, harness jingling.
Harold Keith, *Rifles for Watie*, 1957

Rain and sleet had rattled persistently against the wagon's canvas top all through the gray winter afternoon.
Frank Castle, *Dakota Boomtown*, 1958

The horsemen rode swiftly, a line of them extending across the prairie, a hundred feet or so separating each from his neighbor.
Paul Evan Lehman, *The Tough Texan*, 1958

> He will hold thee, when his passion shall have
> spent its novel force,
> Something better than his dog,
> a little dearer than his horse.
>
> Tennyson, *Locksley Hall*, 1842

Romance

Down in the cellars underneath his house in Cheapside, Thomas Wainstead was instructing his servant Jeffers, on the drawing of good malmsey which would be needed for supper.
Jean Plaidy, *The Goldsmith's Wife*, 1950

I saw her first in moonlight, and it seems to me now, looking backward, that I shall always see her so in the eye of my mind, a cold blue light behind her and her face in shadow.
Lois Edwards, *My Heart in Hiding*, 1951

"Do you know," Matthew Carlton Hazard used to say in happier times, "the earliest chief thing I knew in my life?"
Paul Horgan, *A Distant Trumpet*, 1951

On a fine evening in September Melissa Hallam sat in Kensington Gardens with a young man to whom she had been engaged for three days.
Margaret Kennedy, *Lucy Carmichael*, 1951

I am writing this book because I understand that "revelations" are soon to appear about that great man who was once my husband, attacking his character, and my own.
Joyce Cary, *Prisoner of Grace*, 1952

For two years the great Colonnade with its four rows of pillars like Roman soldiers on parade had cut Basil off from everything that seemed worth while in life.
Thomas B. Costain, *The Silver Chalice*, 1952

They rode at a footpace, side by side, threading a way among the scuppernongs, and Travis Currain studied the neglected vines, deciding what must be done to bring them back to full productivity.
Ben Ames Williams, *The Unconquered*, 1953

A hurricane in the Caribbean Sea, nicknamed Felicity after the whimsical manner of meteorological officers, had made a brief and spectacular appearance as a series of closely packed concentric circles on all the weather charts of the world.
David Beaty, *The Four Winds*, 1954

When Father Bretherton woke he found himself balanced on golden air.
Phyllis Bottome, *The Secret Stair*, 1954

Cecil had a shovel-shaped beard.
Donald Barr Chidsey, *Captain Bashful*, 1955

Captain John Willet-Payne, temporarily without a ship and employed meanwhile at the Admiralty, gave the clerk an amused look.
F.W. Kenyon, *Emma*, 1955

As Thomas Welles approached the news kiosk, he slowed to a saunter.
Nicholas Monsarrat, *Castle Garac*, 1955

John Foraday had always been quiet and imaginative, and this was the only fault his grandmother had found in him.
Thomas B. Costain, *Below the Salt*, 1957

"Father, I will not marry a bastard!"
Noel B. Gerson, *The Conqueror's Wife*, 1957

I was thirteen and a half, and in one of the lower classes of St. Paul's School, when the magic of the great classical English novelists—Fielding, Smollett, Dickens, Thackeray—suddenly lassoed and enslaved me.
Ernest Raymond, *The Old June Weather*, 1957

"Are you asleep, Jane?"
D.E. Stevenson, *Anna and Her Daughters*, 1958

Nothing spoils a romance
so much as a sense of humour in the woman.

Oscar Wilde, *A Woman of No Importance*, 1893

All history, so far as it is not supported by contemporary evidence, is romance.

Samuel Johnson in Boswell's *Tour to the Hebrides*, 1936

Our Life in the 1960s

Events:

* In 1963, President John F. Kennedy was assassinated; L.B. Johnson then became president.
* Kennedy's brother, Robert, and Martin Luther King, Jr. were both killed in 1968.
* President Kennedy's widow, Jacqueline, married Aristotle Onassis, 1968.
* In the mid-60s, the Vietnam War was raging, while in the States students protested.
* Mao led Cultural Revolution in China.
* Walter Cronkite was our favorite newscaster.
* Mickey Mantle hit his 500th home run.
* Astronaut Neil Armstrong walked on the moon.

Entertainment:

* In 1962, the Beatles revolutionized rock and roll.
* Laugh-In was a TV comedy hit.
* Other popular TV shows were My Favorite Martian, Star-Trek, and The Carol Burnett Show.
* Star-Trek (TV)
* Johnny Carson took over the Tonight Show, 1962.
* The Carol Burnett Show
* Early '60s had Chubby Checker singing about The Twist. By the end of the decade, The Rolling Stones's style was in.
* Charles Schulz's Peanuts comic strip was syndicated.

Films:

* Hitchcock's
    The Birds
    Psycho
* Whatever Happened to Baby Jane?
* The Sound of Music
* Bonnie and Clyde
* Goldfinger
* 2001: A Space Odyssey
* Born Free
* Butch Cassidy and the Sundance Kid
* Midnight Cowboy
* The Lion in Winter
* Lawrence of Arabia
* The Hustler
* The Guns of Navarone

Culture:

* Carl Sandburg
* Andy Warhol

Notable:

* *Time* magazine asked "Is God Dead?"
* Psychedelic rebellion, hippies, and drugs led to the musical Woodstock Festival 1969.
* Catholics were first allowed to eat meat on Fridays
* Betty Freidan's *The Feminine Mystique*
* Ralph Nader's *Unsafe at Any Speed*
* Erik Erikson's psychobiography *Gandhi's Truth*
* Scientists characterize quasars

Mystery

The case began quietly, on the women's floor of the county jail.
Ross Macdonald, *The Ferguson Affair*, 1960

They thought she was colored at first.
Ed McBain, *The Empty Hours*, 1960

At the moment that Hernando Sotomayor became the late Senor Sotomayor, only four persons knew that he had been murdered.
Wade Miller, *Sinner Take All*, 1960

Sometimes the hot night wind brings bad dreams.
John D. MacDonald, *Where is Janice Gantry?* 1961

Miss Jane Marple was sitting by her window.
Agatha Christie, *The Mirror Crack'd*, 1962

In the quiet room a shot rang out.
Anthony Gilbert, *No Dust in the Attic*, 1962

Exactly three months before the killing at Martingale Mrs. Maxie gave a dinner party.
P.D. James, *Cover Her Face*, 1962

If I had dreamed that what I was doing would get me involved with the Sacramento Police Department, particularly with Captain Rose and Sgt. Huber, I wouldn't have been walking south on Third Street that sunny May morning.
Don Blunt, *Dead Giveaway*, 1963

Marrakech is just what the guidebooks say it is.
Len Deighton, *Horse Under Water*, 1963

At approximately ten-forty-five, Della Street nervously began looking at her wrist watch.
Erle Stanley Gardner, *The Case of the Stepdaughter's Secret*, 1963

Across the tracks there was a different world.
Dorothy B. Hughes, *The Expendable Man*, 1963

Theoretically a policeman, like a priest, should be above politics, or at least untouched by party politics, yet it is the policeman who is responsible for enforcing the laws made by the politicians.
J.J. Marric, *Gideon's Vote*, 1964

In his senior year at college Hamilton Mack was voted "the man whose personality was most likely to split."
Harold Q. Masur, *Make a Killing*, 1964

A smear of fresh blood has a metallic smell.
John D. MacDonald, *A Deadly Shade of Gold*, 1965

She worked in one of those Park Avenue buildings which tourists feel obligated to photograph.
John D. MacDonald, *Nightmare in Pink*, 1965

The Turks have dreary jails.
Lawrence Block, *The Thief Who Couldn't Sleep*, 1966

The under sides of the trees were awash in light.
Charlotte Armstrong, *The Lemon in the Basket*, 1967

The heart of London is large; to some it is warm, to others, perhaps to very many others, it is as cold as ice.
John Creasey, *A Bundle for the Toff*, 1967

Friday the nineteenth of May was a full day.
Donald Westlake, *God Save the Mark*, 1967

The alarm went off at six; Dutheil got up at quarter past, obeying movements long since formalized into a ritual.
Nicholas Freeling, *This is the Castle*, 1968

The call came while I was trying to persuade a lameduck Congressman to settle his tab before he burned his American Express card.
Ross Thomas, *Cast a Yellow Shadow*, 1967

The rain was falling in a sweet relentless fashion as it does in spring in London and it was all very peaceful and pleasant, if uncompromisingly wet.
Margery Allingham, *Cargo of Eagles*, 1968

"When does he intend to make an honest woman of you?"
Rae Foley, *Nightmare House*, 1968

The hospital was exactly like any other hospital—green and white and hygienic and profoundly depressing under a veneer of brisk jollity.
Patricia Moyes, *Death and the Dutch Uncle*, 1968

London was having one of her days.
Margery Allingham, *The Allingham-Case Book*, 1969

It was still dark, the middle of the night, it seemed, when the whistles began to blow, a far-off sound at first that Marcy could almost shut out by burrowing into her pillow.
Doris Miles Disney, *Two Little Children and How They Grew*, 1969

They were watching Ryan beat up the Mexican crew leader on 16mm Commercial Ektachrome.
Elmore Leonard, *The Big Bounce*, 1969

Detective Bert Kling went outside to throw up.
Ed McBain, *Shotgun*, 1969

> Many authors have used the pseudonym Nicholas Carter, but Frederick Van Rensselaer Dey wrote the greatest number in that name.

> Genius is one percent inspiration
> and ninety-nine percent perspiration.
> Thomas Alva Edison, *Life*, 1932

Science Fiction

"I've got to get out," Hal Yarrow could hear someone muttering from a great distance.
Philip Jose Farmer, *The Lovers*, 1961

Once upon a time when the world was young there was a Martian named Smith.
Robert Heinlein, *Stranger in a Strange Land*, 1961

"What's it going to be then, eh?"
Anthony Burgess, *Clockwork Orange*, 1962

When an explosion takes place lots of bits and pieces fly all over the scenery.
Eric Frank Russell, *The Great Explosion*, 1962

Jinn and Phyllis were spending a wonderful holiday in space, as far away as possible from the inhabited stars.
Pierre Boulle, *Planet of the Apes*, 1963

His head unnaturally aching, Barney Mayerson woke to find himself in an unfamiliar bedroom in an unfamiliar conapt building.
Philip K. Dick, *The Three Stigmata of Palmer Eldritch*, 1964

I was busy with the Martian mail which had just arrived when the message from Brett Gryce reached me.
Ray Cummings, *Explorers into Infinity*, 1965

In the week before their departure to Arrakis, when all the final scurrying about had reached a nearly unbearable frenzy, an old crone came to visit the mother of the boy, Paul.
Frank Herbert, *Dune*, 1965

It was an old plane, a four-engine plasma jet that had been retired from active service, and it came in along a route that was neither economical nor particularly safe.
Isaac Asimov, *Fantastic Voyage*, 1966

The hour the story begins is known.
Robert Crichton, *The Secret of Santa Vittoria*, 1966

It seemed as I tossed and turned far into the night, maddened by a dripping tap I was too irresolute to fix, that I owed too many people too many things.
Christopher Hodder-Williams, *The Egg-Shaped Thing*, 1967

The creature halted, crouched low against the ground, staring at the tiny points of light that lay ahead, burning softly through the darkness.
Clifford D. Simak, *The Werewolf Principle*, 1967

North of Appalachia an outcropping of wilderness survived.
Piers Anthony, *Omnivore*, 1968

The Right Honourable Zadkill F. Obomi could feel the weight of the night pressing on his grey-wire scalp like the oppressive bulky silence of a sensory deprivation tank.
John Brunner, *Stand on Zanzibar*, 1968

The drought had lasted now for ten million years, and the reign of the terrible lizards had long since ended.
Arthur C. Clarke, *2001: A Space Odyssey*, 1968

A merry little surge of electricity piped by automatic alarm from the mood organ beside his bed awakened Rick Deckard.
Philip K. Dick, *Do Androids Dream of Electric Sheep?*, 1968
(Filmed as Bladerunner)

Lessa woke, cold.
Anne McCaffrey, *Dragonflight*, 1968

Astronauts hold few charms for psychiatrists.
John Boyd, *The Rakehells of Heaven*, 1969

"Crap."
Martin Caidin, *The Mendelov Conspiracy*, 1969

It was news at the time.
L.P. Davies, *Genesis Two*, 1969

From two hundred thousand feet, the surface of the earth below was void of all but the largest geographical features.
Joe Poyer, *North Cape*, 1969

In spite of all his efforts, Tavernor was unable to remain indoors when it was time for the sky to catch fire.
Bob Shaw, *The Palace of Eternity*, 1969

The lamasery rose steeply from the top of the bluff on the Marin County side of the Golden Gate.
Robert Silverberg, *To Live Again*, 1969

In the chamber at the top of the tower were six individuals: three who chose to call themselves "lords" or sometimes "remedials"; a wretched underling who was their prisoner; and two Garrion.
Jack Vance, *Emphyrio*, 1969

It all began with a small scratch on a time exposure of some star clouds in Saggitarius and its presence was blamed on mishandling or faulty processing.
James White, *All Judgment Fled*, 1968

Below are authors who don't limit their work to one genre.

Author	**Mystery**	**SF**	**Western**
Margery Allingham	X	X	
Poul Anderson	X	X	
Anthony Boucher	X	X	
Alfred Coppel	X	X	
John Creasey	X	X	X
and romance			
Stanley Ellin	X	X	
S.A. Lombino	X	X	
John D. MacDonald	X	X	
Sax Rohmer	X	X	
Robert Silverberg	X	X	
Loren Estleman	X		X
Elmore Leonard	X		X
Bill Pronzini	X		X

Mainstream

It's perverse!
Robert Bolt, *A Man for All Seasons*, 1960

There's no use pretending that Government House architecturally has anything to recommend it at all because it hasn't; it is quite agreeable inside with nice airy rooms and deep-set verandahs, but outside it is unequivocally hideous.
Noel Coward, *Pomp and Circumstance*, 1960

Then there was the bad weather.
Ernest Hemingway, *A Moveable Feast*, 1960

A mighty clap of thunder over west, beyond the Ohio, awakened Micah Heath, the bound boy.
Charles Mercer, *Enough Good Men*, 1960

If I am out of my mind, it's all right with me, thought Moses Herzog.
Saul Bellow, *Herzog*, 1961

The islands that lie to the south of Cape Cod are low and sandy.
Nathaniel Benchley, *The Off-Islanders*, 1961

There are various ways of mending a broken heart, but perhaps going to a learned conference is one of the more unusual.
Barbara Pym, *No Fond Return of Love*, 1961

He sat before the mirror of the second-floor bedroom sketching his lean cheeks with their high bone ridges, the flat broad forehead, and ears too far back on the head, and dark hair curling forward in thatches, and amber-colored eyes wide-set but heavy-lidded.
Irving Stone, *The Agony and the Ecstacy*, 1961

I had even reached the point of wondering if Geraldine Vrevoort's suicide, so long dreaded, might not prove in the event a relief, but like everything else about Geraldine, when it came, it came with a nasty twist.
Louis Auchincloss, *Portrait in Brownstone*, 1962

It was raining and it was going to rain.
John William Corrington, *And Wait for the Night*, 1963

It was my destiny to join in a great experience.
Hermann Hesse, *The Journey to the East*, 1963

"Have you seen the skeleton? I am sitting on it."
Jon Cleary, *The Fall of an Eagle*, 1964

They rode through the lush farm country in the middle of autumn through quaint old towns whose streets showed brilliant colors of turning trees.
Hanna Green, *I Never Promised You a Rose Garden*, 1964

I met Jack Kennedy in November, 1946.
Norman Mailer, *An American Dream*, 1964

I pressed the door gently.
Iris Murdoch, *The Italian Girl*, 1964

Never mind what they tell you on Madison Avenue.
Max Shulman, *Anyone Got a Match?*, 1964

Strangers who arrived during the week supposed they had come to a large city, recently deserted.
Kathleen Winsor, *Wanderers Eastward, Wanderers West*, 1965

I get the willies when I see closed doors.
Joseph Heller, *Something Happened*, 1966

Heaven knows, I never meant any of this to happen.
Richard Powell, *Don Quixote, U.S.A.*, 1966

The temperature hit ninety degrees the day she arrived.
Jacqueline Susann, *Valley of the Dolls*, 1966

I was sitting by the Mississippi at Catfish Bend one hot summer afternoon, thinking about the pleasant times I'd had traveling down the river on the Tennessee Belle, when all of a sudden in the willows just behind me I heard a terrible growling and snorting.
Ben Lucien Burman, *Blow a Wild Bugle for Catfish Bend*, 1967

The barman at The Spotted Wonder public house, between Piccadilly Circus and Leicester Square, was reading an old newspaper cutting about himself.
Arthur LaBern, *Frenzy*, 1967

She was so deeply imbedded in my consciousness that for the first year of school I seem to have believed that each of my teachers was my mother in disguise.
Philip Roth, *Portnoy's Complaint*, 1967

"What sort of reception will we get?"
Jerome Weideman, *Other People's Money*, 1967

In the early summer of 1902 John Barrington Ashley of Coaltown, a small mining center in southern Illinois, was tried for the murder of Breckenridge Lansing, also of Coaltown.
Thornton Wilder, *The Eighth Day*, 1967

I was a child molester.
Joyce Carol Oates, *Expensive People*, 1968

On December 22, 1958, only two days before, they had been safe in London.
Richard Condon, *Mile High*, 1969

A man with binoculars.
Michael Crichton, *The Andromeda Strain*, 1969

The express letter came late in the afternoon.
A.J. Cronin, *A Pocketful of Rye*, 1969

He closed his eyes and in a vivid vision saw his fingers turn to twigs, his arms to branches; he became a reaching pine.
Bruce Lowery, *Werewolf*, 1969

From the sky, there was only a feeling of light.
Eugenia Price, *New Moon Rising*, 1969

Amerigo Bonasera sat in New York Criminal Court Number 3 and waited for justice; vengeance on the men who had so cruelly hurt his daughter, who had tried to dishonor her.
Mario Puzo, *The Godfather*, 1969

Mr. Donnelly the track coach ended the day's practice early because Henry Fuller's father came down to the high-school field to tell Henry that they had just got a telegram from Washington announcing that Henry's brother had been killed in action in Germany.
Irwin Shaw, *Rich Man, Poor Man*, 1969

Western

Here is where I think it begins—with Mr. Henry Mendez, the Hatch and Hodges Division Manager at Sweetmary and still my boss at the time, asking me to ride the sixteen miles down to Delgado's with him in the mud wagon.
Elmore Leonard, *Hombre*, 1961

Brick Gordon's mood was evil, his temper short, and he was well aware of it.
Lynn Westland, *Thunder to the West*, 1964

Frank Shade had traveled a long way to get nowhere.
Clifton Adams, *The Grabhorn Bounty*, 1965

On this dark February day in 1847, the usually placid waters of the Gulf of Mexico were roiling and hissing in angry protest at the harsh onslaught on the rain-filled raging Norther.
Nelson and Shirley Wolford, *The Spring Canyon*, 1965

Jim Beckwith's mustang crested a river of horns.
Carter Travis Young, *Long Boots, Hard Boots*, 1965

The name on the red clapboard depot read Torpedo.
Bill Burchardt, *Yankee Longstraw*, 1965

Shorty Gibbs lay on the gray edge of consciousness, his eyes tightly closed, trying to guess where he was.
Clifton Adams, *Shorty*, 1966

At high noon the stage wheeled precariously around a sharp turn at the top of a barren ridge and began its descent to the desert floor over a series of switchbacks that the driver negotiated with practiced but hair-raising ease.
Lewis B. Patten, *No God in the Saguaro*, 1966

All that day the hard-eyed men had straggled down from Laredo and Hidalgo and a hundred other border crossings that the Mexicans were too busy to patrol.
Clifton Adams, *The Most Dangerous Profession*, 1967

Oklahoma was a raw scar.
Jack M. Bickham, *The War of Charity Ross*, 1967

Martin Robuck, stretching himself by the wagon, inhaled deeply and watched pale light dampled the eastern sky.
Fred Grove, *Buffalo Spring*, 1967

In the Arkansas Ozarks the times weren't easy that war summer of 1861.
Will Henry, *One More River to Cross*, 1967

When they topped the low ridge on their return to the ranch house, Greg Corwin reigned in Hobe Terrall with an over the shoulder look of surprise, pulled his horse half around, bleak eyes narrowing in something like fright and suspicion.
Richard Poole, *Danger Valley*, 1968

The letters informing U.S. Marshall Harvey Sheridan Taggart that he was to expect to welcome and deputize a well-bred, highly-educated young eastern gentleman by the name of Clarence D Peale came close to driving the marshall into armed rebellion against superiors and the government of the United States.
Herbert R. Purdum, *A Hero for Henry*, 1968

The sun twinkled on bright saddle ornaments a mile back of them high on the bare slope.
John Reese, *Sun-Blind Range*, 1968

The horse, a white stocking roan poked its way toward headquarters, pretty much to suit itself.
Giff Cheshire, *Ambush at Bedrock*, 1969

The tobiana mare might be a little long in the tooth, but she had a smooth, easy single-foot that she could hold all day.
Lee Hoffman, *Loco*, 1969

The hunters had become the hunted!
Tex Steele, *Texas Rebellion*, 1969

Zack Maberly sat with the scrubbed surface of the kitchen table between him and the girl.
William O. Turner, *Maberly's Kill*, 1969

Go west, young man, go west.
John L. Soule, *Terre Haute Express*, 1851.

Romance

"Well, frankly it was an accident," Edie Barlow's sister said to her as they sat together over the remains of veal scaloppini.
David Delman, *A Time to Marry*, 1961

"There is a dead horse lying in the street," she said.
Vina Delmar, *The Big Family*, 1961

After eight years in his own professionally-decorated office on the upper East Side, Dr. Spencer Fifield had an internal-medicine practice that consisted of a nice proportion of businessmen and their wives, plus a rather large assortment of what Spencer's colleagues referred to as "Fifield's screwballs."
Lillian Ross, *Vertical and Horizontal*, 1963

Berenice was sixteen years old when she witnessed her father's murder, and she watched the sequence of events that led to it with curious indifference.
Howard Fast, *Agrippa's Daughter*, 1964

How unused, Carlotta pondered irresponsibly, Americans had become to crooked teeth in the young.
Cecily Crowe, *The Tower of Kilraven*, 1965

Martha Ingram had come to Rome to escape something; George Hartwell had been certain of it from the first.
Elizabeth Spencer, *Knights and Dragons*, 1965

Somebody once wrote something, Anabella Baird reflected, about every prospect pleasing and only man being vile.
Elizabeth Cadell, *The Fox From His Lair*, 1966

If anybody cares to read a simple tale told simply, I John Ridd, of the parish of Oare in county of Somerset Yeoman and church warden have seen and had a share in some doing of this neighborhood which I will try to set down in order, God sparing my life and memory.
Richard D. Blackmore, *Lorna Doone*, 1967

While waiting in the old house in Copenhagen, Det Gamle Huus, as the Danes would call it, with a fire crackling on the wide hearth and a gale sweeping up the Sound so that flying spume clouded the windows, I decided to write my autobiography.
Dorothy Eden, *The Shadow Wife*, 1967

The shop, discreet and unostentatious as it appeared from the outside, was one of the most famous in the world.
Emilie Loring, *A Key to Many Doors*, 1967

Once upon a time I had two great loves—Ruebens and the theater.
Ernest Borneman, *The Man Who Loved Women*, 1968

The town of Tilton was by no means as inaccessible as the summit of Mount Everest.
Elizabeth Corbett, *Ladies Day*, 1968

It doesn't take them long to call you a whore, a woman from the gutter.
Alberto Berilacqua, *Califfa*, 1969

Often he thought: My life did not begin until I knew her.
Evan S. Connell, Jr., *Mr. Bridge*, 1969

On the eve of her seventh birthday Annabella Lagrange learned that it was wrong for men to ask a penny a day more for twelve hours' work down a coal mine and also that because of such wrongdoing they were deprived of food and shelter.
Catherine Cookson, *The Glass Virgin*, 1969

Suddenly he became again the boy in the gardens of the crematorium sixteen years ago and again Eve said, "Come to *us* if you like."
Sumner Locke Elliott, *Edens Lost*, 1969

When Oliver saw his sister in her bridesmaid's dress he laughed so much he could hardly stand.
Elizabeth Jane Howard, *Something in Disguise*, 1969

Rejections

* John Creasey wrote 564 books under his 13 pseudonyms. He received over 700 rejection letters before a publisher accepted one of his novels.
* James Joyce snared over twenty rejections on *Dubliners*.
* Pearl S. Buck's *The Good Earth* received twelve rejections.

Our Life in the 1970s

Events:

* During Richard M. Nixon's second term as president, after the 1974 Watergate scandal he resigned.
* President Carter pardoned U.S. draft evaders in 1977.
* Margaret Thatcher became the first woman British Prime Minister.
* Prime Minister Pierre Trudeau worked to keep Canada's unity when Quebec rebelled.
* Anwar Sadat was elected President of the United Arab Republic.
* Sadat and Israel's Prime Minister Begin were jointly awarded the Nobel Peace Prize.
* Accused racist Alabama Governor George Wallace was shot and partially paralyzed in 1972.
* The Supreme Court legalized abortion.

Entertainment:

* Charlie's Angels (TV)
* All in the Family (TV)
* M*A*S*H* (TV)

Films:

* Sleeper
* True Grit
* Catch-22
* The French Connection
* Last Tango in Paris
* The Sting
* Jaws
* Rocky
* Taxi Driver
* Saturday Night Fever
* Star Wars
* Superman

Culture:

* Alex Haley's *Roots*
* Jesus Christ: Superstar
* Theorode Roszak's *The Making of a Counterculture*
* Robert Moog patented his synthesizer

Notable:

* Three Mile Island (Pennsylvania) nuclear accident
* Rings of Uranus were discovered.
* Scientists determine, from a meteorite, that elements exist for life in outer space.
* Bone tool found, dating life at 27,000 B.C.
* National Organization for Women represented goals for women.
* The first non-Italian in 500 years was named Pope.
* Cigarette commercials banned from TV, 1971.
* Gas shortage in the U.S. caused a long wait at the pumps.
* Bing Crosby passed away.

Mystery

In Devon's dream they were searching the reservoir again for Robert.
Margaret Millar, *Beyond this Point are Monsters*, 1970

The debriefing took ten days in a sealed-off suite in the old section of the Army's Letterman General Hospital on the Presidio in San Francisco and when it was finished, so was my career—if it could be called that.
Ross Thomas, *The Fools in Town are on Our Side*, 1970

Barnaby Grant looked at the Etruscan Bride and Bridegroom who reclined so easily on their sarcophagal couch and wondered why they had died young and whether, as in Verona, they had died together.
Nagio Marsh, *When in Rome*, 1971

Detective Steve Carella wasn't sure he had heard the man correctly.
Ed McBain, *Sadie When She Died*, 1972

They were old hundred-dollar bills, a little limp now, even a little greasy, and one of them had a rip in it that somebody had neatly mended with a strip of Scotch tape.
Ross Thomas, *The Porkchoppers*, 1972

First, I closed the windows and bolted the flimsy aluminum door.
Charles Willeford, *Cockfighter*, 1972

It was one of those jobs you take on when things are very lean.
Bill Pronzini, *Undercurrent,* 1973

It began the way that the end of the world will begin, with a telephone call that comes at three in the morning.
Ross Thomas, *If You Can't Be Good*, 1973

Sleeping fitfully, a big man bulging out of T-shirt and shorts, I wander through a dream where I'm a stranger seeking some palpable reality, a cry on my lips: Where the hall am I?
Andrew Coburn, *The Trespassers,* 1974

He could not get used to going to the girl's apartment.
Elmore Leonard, *52 Pick-up*, 1974

It was a fine night for strolling, but Gabriella Constante hurried.
Lillian O'Donnell, *Dial 577 R-A-P-E*, 1974

There was a white patrol car parked at the curb outside the house.
Ed McBain, *Goldilocks*, 1976

The cellar was divided into rooms.
Ruth Rendell, *A Demon in My View*, 1976

He sat perfectly still in front of the television set in room 932 of the Biltmore Hotel.
Mary Higgins Clark, *A Stranger is Watching*, 1977

Mary Kate Donovan was scared stiff, but she'd rather die than show it.
Stanton Forbes, *Buried in So Sweet a Place*, 1977

The dark-haired man stared at the wall in front of him.
Robert Ludlum, *The Chancellor*, 1977

Ryder opened his tired eyelids and reached for the telephone without enthusiasm.
Alistair MacLean, *Goodbye California*, 1977

Saturday A.M. It was a thin scream; the empty street and the night silence briefly nurtured it, then it was sucked up between the high-rise buildings like smoke up a flue and wafted away across a starless sky.
Lillian O'Donnell, *After-Shock*, 1977

When I finally caught up with Abraham Trahearne, he was drinking beer with an alcoholic bulldog named Fireball Roberts in a ramshackle joint just outside of Sonoma, California, drinking the heart right out of a fine spring afternoon.
James Crumley, *The Last Good Kiss*, 1978

On Wall Street grief does not drape city lampposts in black.
Emma Lathen, *Double Double Oil & Trouble*, 1978

"My wife," John Wright said with a start, realizing he had lost track of her.
Andrew Coburn, *The Babysitter*, 1979

If it had been up to Katie Chave she would have called in sick that morning.
Lillian O'Donnell, *No Business Being a Cop*, 1979

Science Fiction

He felt like a mummy awakening from a thousand-year sleep.
Edward W. Ludwig, *The Mask of Jon Culon*, 1970

His wife had held him in her arms as if she could keep death away from him.
Philip Jose Farmer, *To Your Scattered Bodies Go*, 1971

Sooner or later, it was bound to happen.
Arthur C. Clarke, *Rendevois with Rama*, 1973

Ziantha stood before the door smoothing a tight-fitting glove with her other hand.
Andre Norton, *Forerunner Foray*, 1973

On the night he had chosen months before, Malacar Miles crossed the street numbered seven, passing beneath the glow-globe he had damaged during the day.
Roger Zelazny, *To Die in Italbar*, 1973

...and there it is!
John Brunner, *Total Eclipse*, 1974

Hugh Valleroy paced back and forth, heedless of the muddy water he was splashing onto the boots of the District Director of Federal Police.
Jacqueline Lichtenberg, *House of Zeor*, 1974

"I tell you I still don't like it," Peder Forbarth said nervously.
Barrington J. Bayley, *The Garments of Caean*, 1976

There were three of them, although sometimes there was only one of them.
Clifford D. Simak, *Shakespeare's Planet*, 1976

A bright flash of insight, to match that peculiar sun...
Roger Zelazny, *The Hand of Oberon*, 1976

When Menolly, daughter of Yanus Sea Holder, arrived at the Harper Craft Hall, she came in style, aboard a bronze dragon.
Anne McCaffrey, *Dragonsinger*, 1977

Close your eyes.
Joe Haldeman, *All My Sins Remembered,* 1977

One of the curious customs to arise out of the collapse was the practice of pyramiding robotic brain cases, in the same manner that certain ancient asiatic barbarians raised pyramids of human heads that later turned to skulls, to commemorate a battle.
Clifford D. Simak, *A Heritage of Stars*, 1977

Seven misshapen figures emerged from a blinding swirl of desert sand and sage.
Steven Spielberg, *Close Encounters of the Third Kind*, 1977

Sven Evenson stood looking up at the small landing craft as it made its swift descent from the orbiting spaceship toward the open space in front of him.
Arthur Tofte, *Survival Planet*, 1977

"At first, they were saying about him, Oh, my God. It's Hitler all over again!"
William F. Buckley, Jr., *Stained Glass*, 1978

Dirshan was a dead man.
Gene Lancour, *Sword for the Empire*, 1978

In the sunlight in the center of a ring of trees Lev sat cross-legged, his head bent above his hands.
Ursula Leguin, *The Eye of the Heron*, 1978

As the graveyard shift at Mission Control approached the seven A.M. changeover, the satellite communications section was quiet.
Geoffrey Simmons, *The Adam Experiment*, 1978

Most of the bodies were near the silos and storage tanks, where the defenders had retreated in the end.
Chelsea Quinn Yarbro, *False Dawn*, 1978

"Rocky, would you take a look at this?"
John Varley, *Titan*, 1979

Life goes on yes—any fool and his self-respect are soon parted perhaps never to be reunited, even on Judgment Day.
Kurt Vonnegut, *Jailbird*, 1979

Pseudonym Quiz: Science Fiction Authors

Match these pen names with their authors. Some of them write under more than one pseudonym, as well as their own names. Answers are on page 88.

Pseudonym

1. Calvin M. Knox
2. Walker Chapman
3. A.A. Craig
4. Murray Leinster
5. John Riverside
6. Edward Banks
7. Leonard Douglas
8. Walter Drummond
9. George E. Dale
10. Leonard Spaulding
11. D.R. Banat
12. William Anthony Parker White
13. Sax Rohmer
14. Rog Phillips
15. Caleb Saunders
16. Lyle Monroe
17. Christopher Bush
18. Winston P. Sanders
19. William Elliott
20. Lee Sebastian
21. Ivar Jorgenson
22. Anson Macdonald
23. Michael Karageorge
24. Charles Beaumont
25. C.J. Cherryh
26. Voltaire

Author Name

a. Robert Silverberg
b. Roger Phillips Graham
c. Robert A. Heinlein
d. David Osborne
e. Anthony Boucher
f. Charles Christmas Bush
g. Arthur Sarsfield Ward
h. Ray Bradbury
i. Isaac Asimov
j. William Fitzgerald Jenkins
k. Poul Anderson
l. Charles Nutt
m. Francois-Marie Arouet
n. Carolyn Janice Cherry

Mainstream

I am an old man now, but then I was already past my prime when Arthur was crowned King.
Mary Stewart, *The Crystal Cave*, 1970

Not to every young girl is it given to enter the harem of the Sultan of Turkey and return to her homeland a virgin.
Dorothy Dunnett, *The Ringed Castle*, 1971

"What is your name?"
John Hawkesworth, *Upstairs Downstairs*, 1971

Mother Hirsch was asleep when the taxi pulled to the curb.
Zelda Popkain, *A Death of Innocence*, 1971

The primroses were over.
Richard Adams, *Watership Down*, 1972

Chesser had come to London ten times a year for the past ten years.
Gerald A. Browne, *11 Harrowhouse*, 1972

There were 117 psychoanalysts on the Pan Am flight to Vienna and I'd been treated by at least six of them.
Erica Jong, *Fear of Flying*, 1973

The old woman's head was barely fretting against the pillow.
Patrick White, *The Eye of the Storm*, 1973

It is said we have ten seconds when we wake of a morning, to remember what it was we dreamed the night before.
Richard Bach, *A Gift of Wings*, 1974

Early in the spring of 1750, in the village of Juffure, four days upriver from the coast of The Gambia, West Africa, a manchild was born to Omoro and Binta Kinte.
Alex Haley, *Roots*, 1974

The main entrance to Falconer—the only entrance for convicts, their visitors, and the staff—was crowned by an escutcheon representing Liberty, Justice and, between the two, the sovereign power of government.
John Cheever, *Falconer*, 1975

It was like he was doing me a favor taking me to this place.
Judith Rossner, *Looking for Mr. Goodbar*, 1975

She felt the snake between her breasts, felt him there, and loved him there, coiled, the deep tumescent S held rigid, ready to strike.
Harry Crews, *A Feast of Snakes*, 1976

To have a reason to get up in the morning, it is necessary to possess a guiding principle.
Judith Guest, *Ordinary People*, 1976

In these days cheap apartments were almost impossible to find in Manhattan, so I had to move to Brooklyn.
William Styron, *Sophie's Choice*, 1976

I recall with utter clarity the first great shock of my life.
Leon Uris, *Trinity*, 1976

As the carriage drew away from the Circular Wharf Mr. Stafford Merivale tapped the back of his wife's hand and remarked that they had done their duty.
Patrick White, *A Fringe of Leaves*, 1976

Nancy Greeney lay on ther operating table on her back, staring up at the large kettle-drum shaped lights in operating room number 8, trying to be calm.
Robin Cook, *Coma*, 1977

Every old house, during a long association with human misfortune, acquires a ghost; the chateau of Chenonceaux is haunted by a queen of France.
David Linzee, *Discretion*, 1977

The bus, because of the unevenness of the road, lurched and swayed so that the old man sitting across the way from Sister Luiza had trouble with his eating.
Victor Canning, *Birdcage*, 1978

Something disturbed Marissa Blumenthal.
Robin Cook, *Outbreak*, 1978

Colonel Helmut von Schraeder surveyed the lobby of the old hotel as he gently tugged his gloves free.
Robert L. Fish, *Pursuit*, 1978

They say I'm dead.
Herbert Lieberman, *The Climate of Hell*, 1978

The sea which lies before me as I write glows rather than sparkles in the bland May sunshine.
Iris Murdock, *The Sea, The Sea*, 1978

By the time he graduated from college John Smith had forgotten all about the bad fall he took on the ice that January day in 1953.
Stephen King, *The Dead Zone*, 1979

Mr. van Haagen glanced about the table at Gad's and said benevolently, meaning well, "It is not often that one has the happiness of seeing so many old faces after so few years."
Norah Lofts, *The Haunting of Gad' s Hell*, 1979

Because he thought that he would have problems taking the child over the border into Canada, he drove south, skirting the cities whenever they came and taking the anonymous freeways which were like a separate country as travel was itself like a separate country.
Peter Straub, *Ghost Story*, 1979

Pseudonym Quiz: Mainstream Authors

Match these pen names with their authors. Answers are on page 88.

Pseudonym   **Author Name**

1. Mark Twain   a. Roy Vickers
2. Lewis Carroll   b. Samuel Clemens
3. David Durham   c. Francois Marie Aroult
4. S.S. VanDine   d. William Sydney Porter
5. Voltaire   e. Charles LutwidgeDodgson
6. O. Henry   f. Williard Huntington Wright

Truman Capote on the editing process: "I believe more in scissors than I do in the pencil."

Western

A rider passing out of the province from Mexico into the territory of Arizona encounters perhaps as white a terrain as can be found in any desert on earth.
Jay Hayden, *Sonora Pass*, 1970

It was the year 1907: Theodore Roosevelt was president; the city of Los Angeles had a population of more than a quarter of a million, and Jeff Decker had a thirst.
Richard Wormser, *The Ranch by the Sea*, 1970

Gone Tomorrow was a community that had been born only days ago, and soon it would be no more.
Cliff Farrell, *Owl Hoot Trail*, 1971

Sun pounded down on the vast grey-brown rolling plains making a sweltering furnace of the coach from Fort Worth as it swayed and shuddered, bucking over deep impressions in the road.
Harry Sanford and D.C. Fontana, *The Brazos River*, 1971

Leaving Missouri had been a last hope—an admission of defeat—with death stalking the way.
Jay Shane, *They Called Him a Fox with Six-Guns*, 1971

One thing about Montana, you could watch rain coming a long way off.
Carter Travis Young, *The Pocket Hunters*, 1972

The tiny house must have been white at one time, before fierce Kansas summers checked and blistered the paint, and Kansas winters scoured it down to the raw timber.
Dwight Bennett, *The Guns of Ellsworth*, 1973

The train stopped here for exactly two minutes, and by the time Leatherman had swung down off the Pullman and taken his suitcase from the porter, the whistle blasted and it was on its way again.
Richard Meade, *Cartridge Creek*, 1973

They got him between them on the narrow upward trail before he knew what was happening.
John Reese, *They Don't Shoot Cowards*, 1973

From his spot in the sheltering brush beside the trail, Dork Wallace watched the single rider moving forward toward the riverbank.
Todhunter Ballard, *Home to Texas*, 1974

The editor of the Domingo Weekly Observer leaned against the doorjamb and chewed impatiently on an unlighted cigar as he frowned at the lazy street.
Elmer Kelton, *Manhunters*, 1974

Well, preacher, if you've come to pray over me in my last hours, I'm afraid it's too late.
Lee McElroy, *Joe Pepper*, 1975

Whenever he rode into this town—which was every other week or so to report the condition of John Isely's scattered cattle holdings—Will Bonner was sure the place had grown since last time.
Dwight Bennett, *The Cheyenne Encounter*, 1976

I folded the russet pelisse and placed it near my travel bag.
Helen York, *Tremorra Towers*, 1976

There were parts of Kansas City where you could get your head caved in or your ribs parted by a sharp knife in broad daylight.
John Reese, *The Cherokee Diamondback*, 1977

Those three old boys were pushing at me, and I couldn't figure why they would.
Frank Roderus, *33 Brand*, 1977

Chase Dalton emptied the bottle and scowled at the half-filled glass.
Giles A. Lutz, *The Turnaround*, 1978

He took one last look at Adam Burgess slumped forward in his chair, his chin resting upon the hilt of the knife in his throat, then quietly closed the door and moved with unhurried footsteps along the carpeted hallway.
Max von Kreisler, *Stand in the Sun*, 1978

The train was still several miles down the track approaching at a brisk, rhythmic pace.
Pabechko Hawkes, *Indians*, 1979

The vaquero named Jaime Ortega unsaddled the grulla and shoved him into the mesquite corrals without currying the animal.
Richard S. Wheeler, *Beneath the Blue Mountain*, 1979

Romance

It's a dismal, cloudy November morning and I'm glad my sister Julia is staying with me; I mind morning weather.
Ellin Berlin, *The Best of Families*, 1970

Sunburned and stripped to shorts, Jack crossed to the bedroom wall switch.
Doris Betts, *The River to Pickle Beach*, 1972

"What the devil am I to do!"
Barbara Cartland, *The Daring Deception*, 1973

Laci awakened.
Nicolas Fokker, *The Tamer*, 1973

In the spring of 1971, when it became apparent to Howard W. Amberson that neither he nor his wife had much time remaining, he walked to Woolworth's and purchased a large ledger, bound in red and gray.
Don Robertson, *Praise the Human Season*, 1974

My face no longer hurt much, but it was still a little swollen on one side from the slapping Strabo had given me the night before.
Madeleine Brent, *Stranger at Wildings*, 1975

The planning of her wardrobe and the subject of clothes had never, for Valle Montgomery, occupied more than a tiny, unregarded corner of her mind.
Joan Aiken, *Castle Barebane*, 1976

BOAC flight 982 was on the final, Beirut-London leg of its trip from Calcutta.
Jonathan Black, *Ride the Golden Tiger*, 1976

"You can like it or lump it," Miss Brown, the dragon in the outer office, spoke emphatically.
Margaret Pargeter, *Stormy Rapture*, 1976

The gravestones were black.
Elizabeth Peters, *Legend in Green Velvet*, 1976

My lover came to me on the last night in April with a message and a warning that sent me home to him.
Mary Stewart, *Touch Not the Cat*, 1976

The sun blazed down on the backs of the Negro slaves and the white indentured bond servants.
Jeanne Wilson, *Weep in the Sun*, 1976

It was several hours since the news of his wife's death had reached him and it still seemed unbelievable, it still had the power to shock.
Constance Heaven, *The Queen and the Gypsy*, 1977

When Ellen Wainwright was married to Richard Lancy in July, 1873, the day was so hot that the church doors were left wide open, and towards the end of the ceremony, a stray dog ran in and stood howling in the central aisle.
Mary E. Pearce, *Cast a Long Shadow*, 1977

Jessica eased the big car down the hill between the rows of pines, and suddenly braked to a stop, her breath catching sharply in her throat.
Elaine Bissell, *Women Who Wait*, 1978

The mansion was isolated and Gothic massive, trapped in a wood, grotesque.
William Peter Blatty, *The Ninth Configuration*, 1978

"Never take anything for granted. Fate or the devil has a way of kicking you up the backside when you least expect it," my grandfather used to say in his coarse way, not that it ever treated him so cavalierly and I never realized how right he was until one night in the summer of 1829.
Constance Heaven, *Lord of Ravensley*, 1978

The first severity of mourning was over.
G.M.T. Parsons, *Laura*, 1978

Julien St. Clair, Earl of March, flicked a careless finger over Yvette's plump belly, lay back on the large four-poster bed, and gazed beneath half-closed lids at the dancing patterns cast by the firelight on the opposite wall.
Catherine Coulter, *The Rebel Bride*, 1979

Once my mother phoned me and said, "Oh, why did the mother in your story have to be so slangy?"
Jessamyn West, *The Life I Really Lived*, 1979

Our Life in the 1980s

Events:

* Ronald Reagan was the fortieth president and served 1980-1988; George Bush was then elected.
* John Lennon was killed on a New York street in 1980.
* In 1981 Anwar Sadat was assassinated.
* Jesse Jackson debuted in politics.
* The first woman, Geraldine Ferraro, was nominated as a vice presidential candidate.
* Iran's Ayatollah Khomeni declared the end of 8-1/2-year Holy War with Iraq.
* In 1989 Communism's 28-mile long Berlin Wall separating Europe from the free world was dismantled.
* Ferdinand Marcos left Philippines; Cory Aquino was elected the country's leader.
* In 1985, the disease AIDS became widely recognized.
* In 1986 the *Challenger* space shuttle exploded shortly after takeoff.
* Also in 1986, the Chernobyl nuclear reactor meltdown caused fear worldwide.
* Massive Exxon oil spill in Alaskan waters

Entertainment:

* Gary Larson's The Far Side comics
* Calvin and Hobbes comics
* Erma Bombeck's humorous column was syndicated.
* Music: Police, Madonna, Michael Jackson
* TV: Miami Vice, Dallas, Bill Cosby, MTV
* Last TV episode of M*A*S*H* 1983

Films:

* Raging Bull
* ET
* Gandhi
* Terms of Endearment
* Back to the Future
* Amadeus
* The Killing Fields
* A Passage to India
* The Untouchables
* Who Framed Roger Rabbit?
* Batman
* Indiana Jones and the Last Crusade
* Field of Dreams

Culture:

* Sting
* Benefit concerts: Save the rainforest; combat AIDS
* Winton Marsalis
* Sylvia Plath's *Collected Poems*
* Ravi Batra's *The Great Depression of 1990*

Notable:

* Volcano Mount St. Helen's erupted.
* In 1981 Britain's Prince Charles married Diana.
* Fifty-two Americans were held hostage fourteen months in Iran.
* Life was judged to have begun 3.5 million years ago.
* Sandra Day O'Connor was the first woman appointed to the Supreme Court.
* Natalie Wood and Lucille Ball were among the celebrities who died this decade.
* Personal computers and jogging—passions of the masses.

Mystery

If her mind had not been on the case she had won, Katie might not have taken the curve so fast, but the intense satisfaction of the guilty verdict was still absorbing her.
Mary Higgins Clark, *The Cradle Will Fall*, 1980

The dead girl lay in a twisted sprawl, like something broken and carelessly discarded, among the reeds and bushes that grew along the edge of Lake Cerced.
Bill Pronzini, *Labyrinth*, 1980

He wasn't a small man, but he walked small.
Paula Gosling, *Solo Blues*, 1981

At six minutes past midnight, Tuesday morning, on the way home from a late rehearsal of her stage show, Tina Rvans saw her son, Danny, in a stranger's car.
Dean Koontz, *The Eyes of Darkness*, 1981

There are no hundred percent heroes.
John D. MacDonald, *Cinnamon Skin*, 1982

Troubled faces had begun to look alike to me.
Jonathan Valin, *Day of Wrath*, 1982

Arthur flung the stone with calculated aim.
Patricia Highsmith, *People Who Knock on the Door*, 1983

She was a very old woman dressed entirely in black, and when she fumbled open my inner office door the aluminum tubing of the walker she was leaning on gleamed like nickel steel against the black of her dress.
Loren D. Estleman, *Sugar-Town*, 1984

And now Cynthia was on about her son again; her confounded dream son.
Michael Innes, *Carson's Conspiracy*, 1984

"Never write a novel in the first person," Jack told me.
Donald E. Westlake, *A Likely Story*, 1984

The San Francisco's Tenderloin is a twenty-square block district that contains some of the greatest contrasts in the city.
Marcia Muller, *There's Nothing to Be Afraid Of*, 1985

"Crap," Sergeant Hoke Moseley told his partner, "is the acronym for finding your way around Miami."
Charles Willeford, *New Hope for the Dead*, 1985

When she was quite sure that Willie was dead Zanny began to scream.
B.M. Gill, *Nursery Crimes*, 1986

When I was nine, I fell in love with a girl of twenty named Barbara, who killed herself.
Peter Lovesey, *Rough Cider*, 1986

"What the hell are you doing here, anyway?" said Corporal Sanducci to the waitress, wishing he had time for another cup of coffee.
L.R. Wright, *Sleep While I Sing*, 1986

Later, I found out his name was John Daggett, but that's not how he introduced himself the day he walked into my office.
Sue Grafton, *'D' is for Deadbeat*, 1987

Standing in front of his dresser mirror, the young man pointed the revolver at his reflection.
James W. Hall, *Under Cover of Daylight*, 1987

Every time they got a call from the leper hospital to pick up a body Jack Delaney would feel himself coming down with the flu or something.
Elmore Leonard, *Bandits*, 1987

"This is some mess in here," Monoghan said.
Ed McBain, *Poison*, 1987

Fontana liked to think he wasn't a murderer.
Earl W. Emerson, *Black Hearts and Slow Dancing*, 1988

I shouldn't have taken either case.
Linda Barnes, *The Snake Tattoo*, 1989

The room was still empty.
Tom Clancy, *Clear and Present Danger*, 1989

Mystery Authors' Trademarks

Some authors structure patterns in titles as their hallmarks:

* John D. MacDonald's Travis McGee series used color (*The Deep Blue Goodbye*).
* Sue Grafton is writing through the alphabet (*A is for 'Alibi'*).
* Lilian Braun uses cats (*The Cat Who Wasn't There*).
* Lawrence Block has the burglar series (*The Burglar in the Closet*).
* Philip Atlee has the word contract (*Paper Pistol Contract*).
* Erle Stanley Gardner always used cases (*The Case of the Angry Mourner*).
* Stuart M. Kaminsky uses red (*A Fine, Red Rain*).
* Ed McBain's Matthew Hope series uses nursery rhyme titles (*Jack and the Beanstalk*).
* Craig Rice played on phrases (*My Kingdom for a Hearse*).
* Edward D. Hoch's phrase is The Spy Who... (*The Spy Who Took the Long Route*).

Of course others use their character's name in the title: Heron Carvis (*Miss Seeton Draws the Line*); Leslie Charteris (*Saint Returns*); John Creasey (*Toff and the Terrified Taxman*; *Inspector West at Bay*); G.G. Fickling (*Gun for Honey*); Brett Halliday (*Violent World of Michael Shayne*); MacDonald Hastings (*Cork in the Doghouse*); Alan Hunter (*Gently Does It*); Michael Innes (*Appleby Talking*); H.R.F. Keating (*Inspector Ghote Plays a Joker*); Harry Kemelman (*Sunday the Rabbi Stayed Home*); J.J. Marric (*Gideon's Badge*); Anthony Morton (*Baron and the Unfinished Portrait*); Sax Rohmer (*Re-Enter Fu Manchu*); Georges Simenon (*Maigret and the Headless Corpse*); Arthur W. Upfield (*Bony Buys a Woman*); James Yaffe (*Mom Sings an Aria*).

Science Fiction

Remember to smile a lot, John Renfrew thought moodily.
Gregory Benford, *Timescape*, 1980

"Everybody should fear only one person, and that person should be himself."
Philip Jose Farmer, *The Magic Labrinth*, 1980

The door swung shut silently behind them, cutting off the light, music, and wild celebration of the ballroom.
Joan D. Vinge, *The Snow Queen*, 1980

It was in that year when the fashion in cruelty demanded not only the crucifixion of peasant children, but a similar fate for their pets, that I first met Lucifer and was transported into Hell; for the Prince of Darkness wished to strike a bargain with me.
Michael Moorcock, *The War Hound and the World's Pain*, 1981

"It was in my hair, Severian," Dorcas said.
Gene Wolfe, *The Sword of the Lictor*, 1981

"I don't believe it, of course," said Golan Tervize, standing on the wide steps of Seldon Hall and looking out over the city as it sparkled in the sunlight.
Isaac Asimov, *Foundations' Edge*, 1982

Barefoot conducts his seminars on his houseboat in Sausalito.
Philip K. Dick, *Transmigration of Timothy Archer*, 1982

The gem colored dream shattered and left the kid gaping on the street.
Joan D. Vinge, *Alien Blood*, 1982

Anton huddled in his sheepskin jacket and military-style leather raincoat.
Ian Watson, *Chekhov's Journey*, 1983

The sky above the port was the color of television, tuned to a dead channel.
William Gibson, *Neuromancer*, 1984

"When you finally set yourself alight," Maeve Starzynski said, "don't come crying to me."
Bob Shaw, *Fire Pattern*, 1984

The explosion was utterly silent.
Ben Bova, *Privateers*, 1985

"We need you to kill a man."
Robert A. Heinlein, *The Cat Who Walks Through Walls*, 1985

We slept in what had once been the gymnasium.
Margaret Atwood, *The Handmaid's Tale*, 1986

Ryll felt no pain on awakening and he did not remember the collision.
Frank Herbert and Brian Herbert, *Man of Two Worlds*, 1986

It had already been raining for six days when the enormous shoe washed up onto the beach.
James P. Blaylock, *Land of Dreams*, 1987

Alton Techniksson went to the Morning Gate of Cirque every dawn.
Terry Carr, *Cirque*, 1987

Seamus O'Neill moved his finger to the button to fire the last retrorocket, glanced quickly behind at the inky blackness where the Tps Iona continued its silent orbit.
Andrew M. Greeley, *The Final Planet*, 1987

I am too young to die.
Harry Harrison, *The Stainless Steel Rat Gets Drafted*, 1987

She didn't know she had died.
Michael Swanwick, *Vacuum Flowers*, 1987

In the end there's cruelty and death alone over the land.
Greg Bear, *Eternity*, 1988

The joke in the Starfleet is that the only thing that can travel faster than warp 10 is news.
Diane Duane, *Spock's World*, 1988

At this time John William Washington, who is usually called "Sandy" by his old nursemaid and his six friends, is biologically twenty-two years and eleven months old.
Frederik Pohl, *Homegoing*, 1989

Mainstream

The naked child ran out of the hide-covered lean-to toward the rocky beach at the bend in the small river.
Jean M. Auel, *The Clan of the Cave Bear,* 1980

It was the afternoon of my eighty-first birthday, and I was in bed with my catamite when Ali announced that the archbishop had come to see me.
Anthony Burgess, Earthly Powers, 1980

Honored godfather: with those words I begin the journal I engage myself to keep for you.
William Golding, *Rites of Passage*, 1980

Gynecologists lie.
Gail Parent, *The Best Laid Plans*, 1980

On December 8th, 1915, Meggie Cleary had her fourth birthday.
Colleen McCullough, *The Thorn Birds*, 1982

The large ballroom was crowded with familiar ghosts come to help celebrate her birthday.
Sidney Sheldon, *Master of the Game*, 1982

You better not never tell nobody but God.
Alice Walker, *The Color Purple*, 1982

"There's no barbed wire," said Wendy Lampport, looking along the hedgerow.
Catherine Aird, *Harm's Way*, 1984

At dawn, if it was low tide on the flats, I would awaken to the chatter of gulls.
Norman Mailer, *Tough Guys Don't Dance*, 1984

Trembling with fear, Ayla clung to the tall man beside her as she watched the strangers approach.
Jean M. Auel, *The Mammoth Hunters*, 1985

Of all the rash and midnight promises made in the name of love, none, Boone now knew was more certain to be broken than "I'll never leave you."
Clive Barker, *Cabal*, 1985

In the hospital of the orphanage—the boys' division at St. Cloud's—two nurses were in charge of naming the new babies and checking that their little penises were healing from the obligatory circumcision.
John Irving, *Cider House Rules*, 1985

It was calm and starry at 20,000 feet.
Mike Cogan, *Top Gun*, 1986

The *Cyclops* had less than one hour to live.
Clive Cussler, *Cyclops,* 1986

"You *can't* marry him!"
Pamela Belle, *The Lode Star*, 1987

Ryan was nearly killed twice in half an hour.
Tom Clancy, *Patriot Games*, 1987

The construction crews began work at 7:30, an hour before the doors to the open pavilions opened, two hours before the stores opened.
Ridley Pearson, *The Seizing of Yankee Green Mall*, 1987

She sometimes thought that for her, Nancy Chamberlain, the most straightforward or innocent occupation was doomed to become, inevitably, fraught with tedious complication.
Rosamunde Pilcher, *The Shell Seekers*, 1987

The day before Martin Burney lost his wife Sara he watched her walk away from him, her long hair lifted at the edges by wind from the Atlantic.
Nancy Price, *Sleeping with the Enemy*, 1987

It started with a kid.
Andrew Vachass, *Strega*, 1987

"It might be useful," said the rich, womanly voice, "to model me as your guardian angel."
Andrew M. Greeley, *Angel Fire*, 1988

He stood in the cold outside and to the hinged side of the door so other people could move past him.
Joanne Greenberg, *Of Such Small Differences*, 1988

I'm the vampire Lestat.
Anne Rice, *The Queen of the Damned*, 1988

Maggie and Ira Moran had to go to a funeral in Deer Lick, Pennsylvania.
Ann Tyler, *Breathing Lessons*, 1988

For as long as I could remember, the only person I could share my deepest secrets with was Luke Casteel Jr.
V.C. Andrews, *Gates of Paradise*, 1989

Anna knew that he was doing his best to be interested.
Maeve Binchy, *Silver Wedding*, 1989

"If you want to make a good impression on people, my father used to say, be a listener, not a talker."
Stephen Birmingham, *Shades of Fortune*, 1989

It was perfect.
Leonore Fleischer, *Rain Man*, 1989

People's lives—their real lives, as opposed to their simple physical existences—begin at different times.
Steven King, *The Dalf Half*, 1989

Have you noticed the colors of the spines and covers? Science fiction and mystery uses bright colors. And horror spines are mostly black.

Mark Twain's on publishers: "Take an idiot man from a lunatic asylum and marry him to an idiot woman, and the fourth generation of this connection should be a good publisher from the American point of view."

Western

Cursing as his horse stumbled and went to its knees Dan Ragan kicked free of the stirrups and leaped clear of his saddle.
Ray Hogan, *Ragan's Law*, 1980

Most of the time I stayed clear of towns, preferring my own company and that of some animals to most people, but there are times when I enjoy getting to see some lights and to hear some noises I haven't made myself.
Frank Roderus, *Sheepherding Man*, 1980

There were two flood seasons on the Upper Missouri and Yellowstone.
Robert J. Steelman, *The Great Yellowstone Steamboat Race*, 1980

Hell at its worst couldn't top an Oklahoma summer day.
Giles A. Lutz, *The Great Railroad War*, 1981

Gold!
Larry D. Names, *Boomtown*, 1981

He knew he had let himself go.
William Shambaugh, *Cameron*, 1981

The hearse was drawn by a pair of arrogant-looking matched blacks with coats that shone like stretched satin plumed, bridaled in the appearance of never having been whipped up above a trot.
Loren D. Estleman, *Murdock's Law*, 1982

When the westbound stagecoach skidded to a halt in front of Wolf Springs Emporia Hotel, late that hot summer morning, the off door flung open immediately and a tall, hard-bitten sun-scorched man stepped out into the spinning dust.
Ray Hogan, *The Renegade Gun*, 1982

"Inside, Yank."
Wayne Barton, *Return to Phantom Hill*, 1983

The one room stone jail was pierced by a single small high window.
Dave E. Olson, *Lazlo's Strike*, 1983

There was something wrong at Molly Malone's roadhouse.
Bill Pronzini, *Starvation Camp*, 1984

She looked small standing there and defiantly facing the big man on the horse.
James Wesley, *Bitter Root Showdown*, 1984

Harrison counted the scant handful of coins twice before he wrote down the amount on a deposit slip and entered the amount also in the passbook.
Frank Roderus, *Finding Nevada*, 1985

When stealth means survival, man can outdo a coyote.
Wesley Ellis, *Lone Star and the Timberland Terror*, 1986

The Texas prairie was warm and still for a change, no breeze whatsoever.
Robert E. Trevathan, *Holdup*, 1986

Wade Mattlock lay on the cold ground wishing he had paid closer attention to the old Indian woman's instructions in Kansas.
Johnny Mullins, *Wade's Last Gunfight*, 1987

When Samuel Quarterknight left Helena on Monday June 17, there were three problems fretting his mind.
Bill Pronzini, *The Last Days of Horse-Shy Halloran*, 1987

The voices were muffled through the cracks of the door that led to his parents' bedroom.
Gary D. Svee, *Spirit Wolf*, 1987

It was a great buffalo hunt that year, one of the best in the memory of the People.
Don Coldsmith, *The Medicine Knife*, 1988

You'd think a fellow would learn to take his own advice.
Frank Roderus, *Charlie and the Sir*, 1988

In late summer, Line told him she was two months along.
Glendyn Swarthout, *The Homes Man*, 1988

Clay Hollister rode into Tourneau Flats just as the sun was dropping behind the hills.
Bud Vanzant, *Five Coffins for Hadleyville*, 1989

As he reigned in at the mouth of the canyon, Steve Laughton thought that he was probably riding into a trap.
Clifford Blair, *Devil's Canyon Double Cross*, 1989

Romance

My family hated my job.
Susan Isaacs, *Close Relations*, 1980

"That woman called today."
Helen Van Slyke, *No Love Lost*, 1980

It was a hot June day when I discovered my father's secret which was to change the whole course of my life as well as his.
Victoria Holt, *The Demon Lover*, 1982

The gun was jarringly out of place.
Jacqueline Briskin, *Everything and More,* 1983

Hawke Madison listened absently to his manager enthusiastically reading the names of important guests for the summer, his mind only half on the conversation.
Kay Hooper, *On Wings of Magic*, 1983

The bare semblance of a smile curved Nathan McKendrick's taut lips as he stood at the living room windows looking down at the measured madness in the streets below.
Linda Lael Miller, *Snowflakes on the Sea*, 1984

Everyone agreed it was the grandest and most beautiful wedding in Palm Beach history, but nearly everybody also felt that something was terribly, dreadfully wrong.
Pat Booth, *Palm Beach*, 1985

Carlys Weber Arnold was a woman who never took anything for granted.
Ruth Harris, *Husbands and Lovers*, 1985

The crowd of reporters outside the house in Bel Air parted to let the hearse through.
Michael Korda, *Queenie*, 1985

Audra Crowther sat on the sofa in the living room of her daughter's Manhattan penthouse.
Barbara Taylor Bradford, *Act of Will*, 1986

People who didn't know her thought Miranda was aloof.
Gwen Davis, *Silk Lady*, 1986

When he finally did make love to Greta Garbo, she wore a glove.
Ben Greer, *Time Loves a Hero*, 1986

"Ah," Jennie McCaine groaned sensuously as she settled her slim, sore body into the hot, steaming bath water.
Bobbi Smith, *Arizona Temptress*, 1986

Going to see Clare's family on the isolated hilltop where Ralph Quick had built his domestic fortress was an ordeal for Julia.
Gail Godwin, *A Southern Family*, 1987

Tara had not worn white since her wedding day.
Wilber Smith, *Rage*, 1987

It was almost impossible to get to Lexington and Sixty-third Street.
Danielle Steel, *Fine Things*, 1987

We didn't know we were an odd family.
Caroline Bridgwood, *Trepasses*, 1988

The microphone was shoved into her face.
Catherine Coulter, *False Pretenses*, 1988

Elizabeth Boleyn, who an hour ago had been Elizabeth Howard, shifted her weight from one knee to the other.
Mollie Hardwick, *Blood Royal*, 1988

"Mama," whispered the blond girl in the doorway. "Are you sleeping?"
Carol J. Kane, *Blood and Sable*, 1988

The voluptuous blond woman lifted up on an elbow and pulled a sheet to her breasts.
Judith McNaught, *Something Wonderful*, 1988

The taxi driver thought he had offended me.
Barbara Vine, *The House of the Stairs*, 1988

Nicholas was trying to concentrate on the letter to his mother, a letter that was probably the most important document he would ever write.
Jude Deveraux, *A Knight in Shining Armor*, 1989

"You said you would never go back," Cressida reminded me.
Anna Gilbert, *A Walk in the Wood*, 1989

The most appalling feature of the morning after I nearly committed adultery was my lack of surprise.
Susan Howatch, *Ultimate Prizes*, 1989

Julian Morell's enemies often said he could never quite make up his mind whom he loved more, his mother or himself.
Penny Vincenzi, *Old Sins*, 1989

The most virtuous lady novelists
write things that would make a bartender blush.
H.L. Mencken, *Prejudices: Fifth Series*, 1926.

Women never use their intelligence—
except when they need to prop up their intuition.
Jacques Deval, News summaries, 1954

Pseudonym Quiz: Romance Authors

Match these pen names with their authors. Some of them write under more than one pseudonym. Answers are on page 88.

Pseudonym   **Author Name**

1. Victoria Holt   a. Barbara Mertz
2. Elizabeth Peters   b. Eleanor Burford Hibbert
3. Ursula Torday   c. Paula Allardyce
4. Philippa Carr   d. Jude Gilliam White
5. Jude Deveraux   e. Jeanne Hines
6. Valerie Sherwood
7. Jean Plaidy

"What's the use of their having names," the Gnat said,
"if they won't answer to them?"
Lewis Carroll, *Through the Looking Glass*, 1872

Our Life in the 1990s

Events:
* Saddam Hussein attacked Isreal; the United States launched Operation Desert Storm and became involved in the Persian Gulf War.
* The Nobel Peace Prize was jointly awarded to South Africa's President deKlerk and Nelson Mandela for their achievement of ending apartheid (racial segregation law sanctioned in 1950).
* Ross Perot, 1992 independent presidential candidate, made an impressive showing in this election that democrat Bill Clinton won.
* Janet Reno was the first woman appointed to head the Department of Justice.
* Oklahoma City was bombed.
* Riots erupted in Los Angeles after a jury acquitted four white police officers from beating a black motorist.
* Earthquakes hit Los Angeles as well as Japan.
* Crack cocaine became the most widespread drug problem in the country.
* In a lengthy televised trial, O.J. Simpson was tried and acquitted of the murder of his ex-wife Nicole Brown Simpson and a male friend of hers.
* We continue to pollute our world: air, water, and soil.

Entertainment:
* Dilbert comic strip
* The Simpsons animated cartoon TV show for grownups
* TV's Northern Exposure
* NYPD Blue (TV)

Films:

* Batman Forever
* Apollo 13
* Forrest Gump
* The Silence of the Lambs
* Thelma and Louise
* Jurassic Park
* Unforgiven
* Groundhog Day
* Dances with Wolves
* Terminator 2
* Pretty Woman
* Ghost
* The Lion King

Culture:

* Play: Sunset Boulevard
* Rap music
* Random acts of kindness

Notable:

* Britain's Charles and Diana divorce.
* Corporate downsizing concerns many employees trying to maintain a middle-class lifestyle.
* Johnny Carson terminated his 30 year career hosting The Tonight Show.
* Bill Gates's Microsoft company immensely profitable.
* William Fulbright, Eva Gabor, Jerry Garcia, Rose Kennedy, Mickey Mantle, Dean Martin, Elizabeth Montgomery, Jacqueline Kennedy Onassis, Orville Redenbacher, Ginger Rogers, Jonas Salk, Wolfman Jack (Robert Smith), John Cameron Swayze, Lana Turner, Junior Walker, Evelyn Wood, Roger Zelazny passed away.

Mystery

I accepted a commission that had been turned down by four other writers, but I was hungry at the time.
Dick Francis, *Longshot*, 1990

Most days, I'm all right.
Bill Pronzini, *Jackpot*, 1990

They had been married for thirty-one years, and the following spring, full of resolve and a measure of hope, he would marry again.
Scott Turow, *Burden of Proof,* 1990

It was raining when they rolled me out of the big Lincoln and into the ditch.
Earl W. Emerson, *Yellow Dog Party*, 1991

"A pickle may not remember getting pickled, but that doesn't make it a cucumber."
Linda Barnes, *Coyote*, 1991

Cassie Raintree was dying of brain cancer every afternoon at 2:30.
James W. Hall, *Bones of Coral*, 1991

Saturday, the last day of August I started work before dawn.
Patricia Cornwell, *All that Remains*, 1992

I feel compelled to report that at the moment of death, my entire life did not pass before my eyes in a flash.
Sue Grafton, *"I" is for Innocent*, 1992

A therapist's work is never over.
Jonathan Kellerman, *Private Eyes*, 1992

I awoke on my knees, bound to the bed and spattered with blood from the IV tubes I had pulled free.
Alfred Coppel, *Wars and Winters*, 1993

At first Officer Jim Chee had felt foolish sitting on the roof of the house of some total stranger.
Tony Hillerman, *Sacred Clowns*, 1993

Inside the windowless courtroom, a man awaited sentencing for murder.
Nancy Taylor Rosenberg, *Mitigating Circumstances*, 1993

On the last day of his life he read a warning in his horoscope and cast the newspaper aside when a woman asked if she might share the beach.
Andrew Coburn, *Voices in the Dark*, 1994

The first bullet hit Matthew Hope in the left shoulder.
Ed McBain, *There was a Little Girl*, 1994

When the power went I was finishing a ten-page report.
Sara Paretsky, *Tunnel Vision*, 1994

As often as humanly possible, he tried to put Suzanne out of his mind.
Mary Higgins Clark, *Let Me Call You Sweetheart*, 1995

"Will they see us?" she whispered.
Jonathan Gash, *The Grace in Older Women*, 1995

My decision to become a lawyer was irrevocably sealed when I realized my father hated the legal profession.
John Grisham, *The Rainmaker*, 1995

On the first morning of her husband's lingering death, Lucy Todhunter one day came down to breakfast alone.
Sharyn McCrumb, *If I'd Killed Him When I Met Him*, 1995

For three weeks the young killer actually lived in the walls of an extraordinary 15-room beach house.
James Patterson, *Kiss the Girls*, 1995

Two days after the murder, listening to Brett Allen's tale of innocence and confusion, the lawyer wavered between disbelief and wonder at its richness, so vivid that she could almost picture it as truth.
Richard North Patterson, *The Final Judgment*, 1995

Science Fiction

Maybe returning to New York on the day after he left it had been a mistake.
Poul Anderson, *The Shield of Time*, 1990

Jolie was in France when she felt the pain.
Piers Anthony, *And Eternity*, 1990

Once upon a time there were two cities within a city.
Ray Bradbury, *A Graveyard for Lunatics*, 1990

An angry deity glowered at Alex.
David Brin, *Earth*, 1990

Snow fell in the woods, drifted deep, a pristen starlit world in which a single winter hare made significance—slow advance from a wandering footprinted time past into a white unwritten time to come.
C.J. Cherryh, *Chernevog*, 1990

The tropical rain fell in drenching sheets, hammering the corrugated roof of the clinic building, roaring down the metal gutters, splashing on the ground in a torrent.
Michael Crichton, *Jurassic Park*, 1990

The trouble with an Orphanage upbringing is that when the College discharges you at age eighteen you are burstingly healthy, educated to the edge of intellectual indigestion, and as innocent of day to day reality as a blind dummy.
George Turner, *Brain Child*, 1991

"Touchdown."
Ben Bova, *Mars*, 1992

David Ogden took a long time to die, and he did not die unnoticed.
Herbert Buckholz, *Brain Damage*, 1992

In the corner of a distant galaxy a world winked out.
Louise Lawrence, *Keeper of the Universe*, 1992

I no longer live in the City of Truth.
James Morrow, *City of Truth*, 1992

Robert E. Lee paused to dip his pen once more in the inkwell.
Harry Turtledove, *The Guns of the South*, 1992

"In five years, the penis will be obsolete," said the salesman.
John Varley, *Steel Beach*, 1992

It was the laughter that made her run, more than the dark, more than that gliding shadow.
Whitley Strieber, *Unholy Fire*, 1992

Dusk settled down about the Fourlands, a slow graying of light, a gradual lengthening of shadows.
Terry Brooks, *The Talismans of Shannara*, 1993

She is a Goldenwing and her name is Glory.
Alfred Coppel, *Glory*, 1993

Nick Naylor had been called many things since becoming chief spokesman for the Academy of Tobacco Studies, but, until now, no one had actually compared him to Satan.
Christopher Buckley, *Thank You for Smoking*, 1994

Theodore is in the ground.
Caleb Carr, *The Alienist*, 1994

For some of us, of course, nothing would be enough.
Nancy Kress, *Beggars and Choosers*, 1994

Kibbe gave the rope one last pull.
Anne McCaffrey, *The Dolphins of Pern*, 1994

One day the sky fell.
Kim Stanley Robinson, *Green Mars*, 1994

I am a robot.
Isaac Asimov, *Gold*, 1995

The crow with the red eyes sat on a branch in the towering old white oak where the leafy boughs were thickest and stared down at the people gathered for their picnic in the sunny clearing below.
Terry Brooks, *Witches Brew*, 1995

The bells of St. Mark's were ringing changes up on the mountain when Bud skated over to the mod parlor to upgrade his skull gun.
Neal Stephenson, *The Diamond Age*, 1995

Sometimes Hugh Brenner thought he'd been born on the wrong planet.
James P. Hogan, *Paths to Otherwhere*, 1996

A.D. 1892 Cloud covered the sky like a gray stone plate.
Larry Niven, *The Ringworld*, 1996

Sixteen light years from Earth today, in the fifth month of the voyage, and the silken force of nospace acceleration continues to drive the starship's velocity ever higher.
Robert Silverberg, *Starborne*, 1996

Science Fiction Mysteries

Some authors write for several genre. In these works, authors combined science fiction and mystery.

The Caves of Steel	Lord Darcy series
The Naked Sun	Randall Garrett
The Robots of Dawn	*The Golden Witchbreed*
Isaac Asimov	Mary Gentle
The Demolished Man	*Double Star*
Alfred Bester	Robert Heinlein
The Squares of the City	*The Murder of the U.S.A.*
John Brunner	Will F. Jenkins
Fire, Burn!	*Darkworld Detective*
John Dickson Carr	J. Michael Reaves
Needle	*The Tenth Victim*
Hal Clement	Robert Sheckley
Police Your Planet	
Lester Del Rey	
Do Androids Dream of Electric Sheep?	
Philip K. Dick	
Time and Again	
Jack Finney	

Mainstream

Late in August three crows took up residence in the chimney of the corner house on Hemlock Street.
Alice Hoffman, *Seventh Heaven*, 1990

Stephen was watching the two girls, though they were not aware of it.
Malcolm MacDonald, *A Woman Alone*, 1990

I'm as peaceful a man as you're likely to meet in America now, but this is about a death I may have caused.
Reynolds Price, *The Tongues of Angels*, 1990

Standing amid the tan, excited post-Christmas crowd at the Southwest Florida Regional Airport, Rabbit Angstrom has a funny sudden feeling that what he has come to meet, what's floating in unseen about to land, is not his son Nelson and daughter-in-law Pru and their two children but something more ominous and intimately his: his own death, shaped vaguely like an airplane.
John Updike, *Rabbit at Rest*, 1990

I had seldom felt so drained, so exhausted, both emotionally and physically.
Phyllis A. Whitney, *The Singing Stones*, 1990

"Are you sure this is the right road?"
Anthony Bruno, *Bad Business*, 1991

There are no prizes for guessing almost right.
Gerald Hammond, *Whose Dog Are You?*, 1991

The map under glass made no sense.
Nicholas Jose, *Avenue of Eternal Peace*, 1991

On a late-winter evening in 1983, while driving through fog along the Maine coast, recollections of old campfires began to drift into the March mist, and I thought of the Abnaki Indians of the Algonquin tribe who dwelt near Bangor a thousand years ago.
Norman Mailer, *Harlot's Ghost*, 1991

Ever after, whenever she smelled the peculiar odor of new construction, of pine planking and plastic plumbing pipes, she would think of that summer, think of it as the time of changes.
Anna Quindlen, *Object Lessons*, 1991

Six days ago, a man blew himself up by the side of a road in northern Wisconsin.
Paul Auster, *Leviathan*, 1992

The 727 was lost in a sea of cumulus clouds that tossed the plane around like a giant silver feather.
Sidney Sheldon, *The Stars Shine Down*, 1992

Alex slammed the door as hard as she could, the sound venting some of her irritation.
Phyllis A. Whitney, *The Ebony Swan*, 1992

On the morning of August 8, 1965, Robert Kincaid locked the door to his small two-room apartment on the third floor of a rambling house in Bellingham, Washington.
Robert Waller, *Bridges of Madison County*, 1992

He'd never particularly liked cats.
Sandra Brown, *Where There's Smoke*, 1993

Tom Sanders never intended to be late for work on Monday, June 15.
Michael Crichton, *Disclosure*, 1993

A time came when my wife and my law partners were convinced I was going crazy and the best I could reply was "I hope not."
Clifford Irving, *Final Argument*, 1993

It was going to be a lousy day.
Andrew Klavan, *The Animal Hour*, 1993

"No!" she hears her mother's voice—frantic with a wild edge that scares her.
Carol Brennan, *In the Dark*, 1994

There was a university somewhere in the Midwest, Jack had once heard on the radio, which had an instrument package designed to go inside a tornado.
Tom Clancy, *Debt of Honor*, 1994

By April most people had already forgotten about him, except for some of the nurses on the floor who crossed themselves when they walked past his room.
Alice Hoffman, *Second Nature*, 1994

Jail is not as bad as you might imagine.
Anna Quindlen, *One True Thing*, 1994

He didn't want to be there.
Nora Roberts, *Hidden Riches*, 1994

It had snowed all day.
Anne Rice, *Taltos*, 1994

When I picked up the mail at the post office, I found one first-class envelope in with the usual junk.
Phyllis A. Whitney, *Daughter of the Stars*, 1994

In the Los Angeles Superior Courthouse, at two minutes past 12 I forced my way through a jostling chattering throng of onlookers and rushed to the bathroom, having postponed this necessity throughout the morning's testimony.
Vonnie Comfort, *Denial*, 1995

In 1980, a year after my wife leapt to her death from the Silas Pearlman Bridge in Charleston, South Carolina, I moved to Italy to begin life anew, taking our small daughter with me.
Pat Conroy, *Beach Music*, 1995

For more than two hundred years, the Owens women have been blamed for everything that has gone wrong in town.
Alice Hoffman, *Practical Magic*, 1995

She sits in the corner, trying to draw air out of a room which seemed to have plenty just a few minutes ago and now seems to have none.
Stephen King, *Rose Madder*, 1995

Jerked from a sound sleep Anne Frasier sat bolt upright in bed and listened.
Eugenia Price, *Beauty From Ashes*, 1995

Misery, Mary thought.
David Rabe, *The Crossing Guard*, 1995

The boss was dying.
Erich Segal, *Prizes*, 1995

Quentin Fears never told his parents the last thing his sister Lizzy said to him before they pulled the plug on her and let her die.
Orson Scott Card, *Treasure Box*, 1996

Western

The train was late, but Judd Medicine Hilk didn't know that, nor did he care.
Gary D. Svee, *Sanctuary*, 1990

One thing about boundary lines, Curtis Daniels thought, as he twisted a little in his saddle in an attempt to ease his aching back, they didn't mean a whole hell of a lot when it came to the weather.
L.J. Washburn, *Riders of the Monte*, 1990

It was a filthy place to raise kids.
Terrell L. Bowers, *Tanner's Last Chance*, 1991

Whitney Pierson held a shotgun in both hands as he stood on the off side of the stagecoach as he tooled into Beaverton.
Lauren Paine, *Riders of the Trojan Horse*, 1991

Folks from back East look at you funny when you talk about that sense that tells you when someone is aiming to put a bullet in your back.
Bill Pinnell, *Terror on the Border*, 1991

He came down from the high hills upon a tired horse and hoping he was a few hours ahead of the vigilant posse.
Bob Terrell, *Reluctant Lawman*, 1991

For quite a few weeks now, Dan Willis had known he needed to begin a serious search for a job.
Frederic Bean, *Hard Luck*, 1992

If this is such a gol'dang good idea, how's come we're hiding it from the grown-ups?
Stephen Calder, *Bonanza: The Ponderosa Empire*, 1992

I limped into town.
Robin Gibson, *Ma Calhoun's Boys*, 1992

John Buckner tossed aside the butt of the stogie had been smoking and glanced about.
Ray Hogan, *The Whipsaw Trail*, 1992

In the late afternoon sun, Dan Casey reigned his black stallion to a halt.
Lee Martin, *Revenge at Rawhide*, 1992

The last time Father licked me I was twelve years old.
Richard White, *Mr. Grey*, 1992

It sounded like the echo of a distant rifle.
Stephen Bly, *Standoff at Sunrise Creek*, 1993

Lad Tremble opened his eyes to the half-light before dawn and felt a rush of fear.
H.B. Broome, *Gambler's Luck*, 1993

"Most train robbers ain't smart, which is a lucky thing for the railroads," Call said.
Larry McMurtry, *Streets of Laredo*, 1993

Cody Bailey slouched in a scarred and battered ladderback chair in Silas Bonner's stuffy office, absentmindedly flicking the rowl of his spur.
Stan Wiseman, *Cody's Ride*, 1993

"I am innocent," George Ives said confidently.
Ralph Compton, *The Virginia City Trail*, 1994

It was dawn in the Sierra Madre of Mexico.
Robert J. Conley, *Gerinmo: An American Legend*, 1994

Samuel Wilders's teeth grated together with each bump and jolt of the wagon.
Gary D. Svee, *Single Tree*, 1994

Big Sam Jones mused that if cinders were food he wouldn't feel so hungry.
Richard S. Wheeler, *Goldfield*, 1995

Caleb rubbed his trigger finger smoothly around the inside of the glass lantern chimney, a black smudge of soot collecting on his callused digit.
Mike Blakely, *Too Long at the Dance*, 1996

> Old soldiers, sweethearts, are surest,
> and old lovers are soundest.
> John Webster, *Westward Hoe*, 1607

Romance

He would kill the American.
Mark Berent, *Steel Tiger*, 1990

Frank first laid eyes on Libby Girard at the Sunday matinee a minute before the lights went down.
Joan Hassler, *North of Hope*, 1990

I would not have believed I could cry so much, but I must not cry now.
Jean Stubbs, *Light in Summer*, 1990

"Promise me, Kate, that you won't let this ruin Christmas."
Elizabeth Forsythe, *Hailey Home Free*, 1991

Elizabeth had just turned sixteen when she saw the plantation for the first time.
Julian Green, *The Distant Lands*, 1991

Freak accidents ran in the family.
Karen Karbo, *The Diamond Lane*, 1991

The bastard looked dead.
Peresa Medeiros, *Heather and Velvet*, 1991

It was a lie, but it was not a lie that could do any damage.
Rosie Thomas, *All My Sins Remembered*, 1991

Most of the nuns have been taken away already.
Marius Gabriel, *The Original Sin*, 1992

Tall, red-haired Abigail MacQueen leapt from slick boulder to boulder above the swirl and shift of foaming green water.
Karen Harper, *The Wings of Morning*, 1993

Claire won the lottery on a Wednesday afternoon in May, the same afternoon that Emma graduated from high school, the dog ran away, and the landlord raised the rent.
Judith Michael, *Pot of Gold*, 1993

Bryan DeCourcey Cavanaugh had a chameleon reputation.
Morris West, *The Lovers*, 1993

Awakened with a sudden start, as though someone had touched my shoulder, and I half expected to see Andrew standing over me as I blinked in the dim room.
Barbara Taylor Bradford, *Everything to Gain*, 1994

Insomnia?
Claudia Crawford, *Bliss*, 1994

You can't be happy in this life because of what happened in your past lives.
Jude Deveraux, *Remembrance*, 1994

Eleanor stood before the abbess' oak table, hiding her fear behind the deceptively sweet smile and innocent expression she always assumed in the presence of Authority.
Ellen Jones, *Beloved Enemy*, 1994

They found her in the trash.
Julie Garwood, *For the Roses*, 1995

There had been nothing portentous about that day in June nothing which might have heralded what was to follow: no lunar eclipse, no unexplained lightning, or shadows falling to the wrong side.
Katherine Mosby, *Private Altars*, 1995

On the day of my husband's annual fund-raising gala, I was down by the river liberating rats.
Ann Rivers Siddons, *Fault Lines*, 1995

Someone was watching her.
Catherine Coulter, *The Cove*, 1996

I never was a virgin.
Susan Isaacs, *Lily White*, 1996

A poor beauty finds more lovers than husbands.
George Herbert, *Jacula Prudentum*, 1651

I can find women who have never had one love affair, but it is rare indeed to find any who have had only one.
Francois Alexandre Frederic Duc De LaRochefoucauld-Liancourt , *Maxims*, n.d. (lived 1747-1827)

Who Said That? Game

Play alone and test yourself or play in a group. Which author wrote a particular opening sentence? Earn ten points for each correct answer. The first player to reach 100 points wins the game.

1. The first time I saw Brenda, she asked me to hold her glasses.
a) Philip Roth, *Goodbye Columbus*, 1959
b) John Updike, *Couples*, 1968
c) Ursula Leguin, *The Dispossessed,* 1974

2. Once upon a time I was very lucky and located a sixty-five-foot hijacked motor sailer in a matter of days, after the authorities had been looking for months.
a) John D. MacDonald, *The Lonely Silver Rain*, 1985
b) John Varley, *Mellinium*, 1983
c) Orson Scott Card, *Speaker for the Dead*, 1986

3. The secret service holds much that is kept secret even from very senior officers in the organization.
a) Ian Fleming, *The Man with the Golden Gun*, 1965
b) Ian Watson, *The Flies of Memory*, 1991
c) Ken Follett, *The Eye of the Needle*, 1978

4. When Mr. Bilbo Baggins of Bag Eng announced that he would shortly be celebrating his eleventy-first birthday with a party of special magnificence, there was much talk and excitement in Hobbiton.
a) J.R. Tolkien, *The Fellowship of the Ring*, 1954
b) Mary Stewart, *Touch Not the Cat*, 1976
c) Isaac Asimov, The Naked Sun, 1957

5. There was a wall.
a) Ursula Leguin, *The Dispossessed,* 1974
b) Arthur C. Clarke, *Imperial Earth*, 1976
c) Louis B. Patten, *Red Runs the River*, 1970

6. "I've watched through his eyes, I've listened through his ears, and I tell you he's the one. Or at least as close as we're going to get."
a) Orson Scott Card, *Ender's Game*, 1977
b) Patricia Cornwell, *Cause of Death*, 1996
c) Ben Bova, *Empire Builders*, 1993

7. It was morning, and the new sun sparkled gold across the ripples of a gentle sea.
a) Richard Bach, *Jonathan Livingston Seagull*, 1970
b) Whitley Strieber, *Unholy Fire*, 1992
c) Susan Morrow, *The Moonlighters*, 1966

8. What can you say about a twenty-five year old girl who died?
a) Erich Segal, *Love Story*, 1970
b) Rog Phillips, *The Involuntary Immortals*, 1959
c) Thomas H. Cook, *Breakheart Hill*, 1995

9. Jack Torrance thought: Officious little prick.
a) Stephen King, *The Stand*, 1977
b) Jack Higgins, *The Eagle Has Flown*, 1991
c) Michael P. Kube-McDowell, *Exile*, 1992

10. After the first hundred years, some people stop taking chances.
a) Joe Haldeman, *Buying Time*, 1989
b) Robert Zelazny, *Mad Wand*, 1981
c) Walter Jon Williams, *Rock of Ages*, 1995

11. The summer my father bought the bear, none of us was born—we were even conceived: not Frank, the oldest; not Frannie, the loudest; not me, the next; and not the youngest of us Lilly and Egg.
a) John Irving, *The Hotel New Hampshire*, 1981
b) Sally Beauman, *Dark Angel*, 1990
c) Ward Just, *Ambition and Love*, 1994

12. The rifleman knelt at the shadow notch in the rocky creek-bed muzzle of the 52 Sharp's rifle trained on a grove of post oak trees 400 yards away.
a) Gene Shelton, *Last Gun*, 1991
b) Sandra Brown, *Texas! Chase*, 1991
c) H.B. Broome, *Violent Summer*, 1990

13. Quietly, moving with stealth in spite of his great size, the huge boar silvertip shouldered its way down the chapparal-covered hillside then paused, unmoving as the granite rocks nearby.
a) Larry J. Martin, *Shadow of the Grisly*, 1993
b) Terry C. Johnston, *Dream Catcher*, 1994
c) Terry Kay, *Shadow Song*, 1994

14. When August came out on the porch, the blue pigs were eating a rattlesnake—not a very big one.
a) Larry McMurtry, *Lonesome Dove*, 1985
b) Giles A. Lutz, *Thieves' Brand*, 1981
c) Louis Begley, *The Man Who was Late*, 1993

15. It is Nathan's fault that I became God.
a) Andrew M. Greeley, *God Game*, 1986
b) Celia Brayfield, *Pearls*, 1987
c) David Eddings, *The Hidden City*, 1994

16. The town of Lake Minnesota, lies on the shore against Adam's Hill, looking east across the blue-green water to the dark woods.
a) Garrison Keillor, *Lake Wobegon Days*, 1985
b) Clive Cussler, *Pacific Vortex!* 1982
c) Walter Jon Williams, *Rock of Ages*, 1995

17. Bud Carson was a newcomer to Chandler, Oklahoma, and it showed.
a) Giles A. Lutz, *Thieves' Brand*, 1981
b) Lindsey Davis, *Shadows in Bronze*, 1990
c) Julian Karr, *Something Borrowed, Something Blue*, 1993

18. "I knew what it was when I heard the shots."
a) Edna Buchanan, *Suitable for Framing*, 1995
b) Stuart M. Kaminsky, *Red Chameleon*, 1985
c) Alison Moore, *Synonym for Love*, 1995

19. It was the size of a small house, weighed 9,000 tons, and was moving at 50,000 kilometers an hour.
a) Arthur C. Clarke, *The Hammer of God*, 1993
b) Kurt Vonnegut, *Slaughterhouse Five or The Children's Crusade*, 1969
c) Clifford D. Simak, *Why Call Them Back From Heaven?* 1967

20. When he was nearly thirteen, my brother, Jem, got his arm badly broken at the elbow.
a) Harper Lee, *To Kill a Mockingbird*, 1960
b) Theodore Olsen, *Bitter Grass*, 1967
c) Bill Gulick, *Distant Trails*, 1988

21. Not many people remember Lamprias now in Athens.
a) Mary Renault, *The Mask of Apollo*, 1966
b) Jennifer Blake, *Wildest Dreams*, 1992
c) Gregory Benford, *Furious Gulf*, 1994

22. "What did you make of the new couple?"
a) John Updike, *Couples*, 1968
b) Vernor Vinge, *A Fire upon the Deep*, 1992
c) Susan Johnson, *Sinful*, 1992

23. The train was an hour late reaching Bridge, California, but this was not bad because some days it did not get there at all.
a) John Reese, *Sure-Shot Shapiro*, 1968
b) Michael Svanwick, *Stations of the Tide*, 1991
c) Gene Tuttle, *Enough Rope to Hang*, 1985

24. It was the coldest winter in forty-five years.
a) Ken Follett, *The Eye of the Needle*, 1978
b) Andrew M. Greeley, *Angel Fire*, 1988
c) Mary Higgins Clark, *Loves Music, Loves to Dance*, 1991

25. Once there was a dead man.
a) Larry Niven, *A World Out of Time*, 1973
b) Gene Wolfe, *The Urth of a New Sun*, 1987
c) Anne McCaffrey, *Nerilka's Story*, 1986

26. Duncan Makenzie was ten years old when he found the magic number.
a) Arthur C. Clarke, *Imperial Earth*, 1976
b) Roger Zelazny, *Sign of Chaos*, 1987
c) Isaac Asimov, *Foundation and Earth*, 1986

27. At dusk he rode up a steep ravine and reached a high mountain meadow that he knew well, a place that was sacred to him.
a) William O. Turner, *Medicine Creek*, 1974
b) Carter Travis Young, *Blaine's Law*, 1974
c) Jack Bassett, *Gunsmoke Creek*, 1971

28. "Some of these people *want* to get killed," said Dickie Cruyer as he jabbed the brake pedal to avoid hitting a newsboy.
a) Len Deighton, *Mexico Set*, 1985
b) Sue Grafton, *"E" is for Evidence*, 1988
c) Clive Barker, *Weaveworld*, 1987

29. Rooter was at once the most difficult and the most helpful of the pequeninos.
a) Orson Scott Card, *Speaker for the Dead*, 1986
b) James Blish, *Earthman, Come Home*, 1956
c) Anne McCaffrey, *Dragonsinger*, 1977

30. The cold passed reluctantly from the earth and the retiring fogs revealed an army stretched out on the hills resting.
a) Stephen Crane, *The Red Badge of Courage*, 1952
b) Patricia Matthews, *Love's Sweet Agony*, 1980
c) Elmer Kelton, *The Day the Cowboys Quit*, 1971

31. Air-raid sirens were warbling the end of a practice alert when Bruce came through the train gate at Union Station.
a) Frank G. Slaughter, *Surgeon, U.S.A.*, 1966
b) Richard North Patterson, *Degree of Guilt*, 1992
c) Stephen R. Donaldson, *Forbidden Knowledge*, 1991

32. When at last they found her and took her out of the water I knew I had to go down and look at her.
a) John D. MacDonald, *All These Condemned*, 1954
b) Beth Gutcheon, *Domestic Pleasures*, 1991
c) Lilian Jackson Braun, *The Cat Who Talked to Ghosts*, 1990

33. Nobody thinks about death on a nice spring day.
a) Ed McBain, *Ten Plus One*, 1963
b) Charlotte Tranbarger, *Destiny's Love*, 1983
c) Ross Thomas, *The Porkchoppers*, 1972

34. If they had meant to hire a sexy receptionist, the law firm of Leech, Bemis and Ott had screwed up.
a) Earl W. Emerson, *Poverty Bay*, 1985
b) L.R. Wright, *The Suspect*, 1985
c) Loren D. Estleman, *Silent Thunder*, 1989

35. Jenny began looking for the cabin at dawn.
a) Mary Higgins Clark, *A Cry in the Night*, 1982
b) Lillian O'Donnell, *Casual Affairs*, 1985
c) Judith Greber, *As Good as it Gets*, 1992

36. Cullom rode out of a canyon blackness that was like a massive weight pressing against him on both sides and into a lingering purple dusk.
a) Carter Travis Young, *Blaine's Law*, 1974
b) Gary McCarthy, *Showdown at Snakegrass Junction*, 1978
c) Blaine M. Yorgason, *Massacre at Salt Creek*, 1979

37. "Why did I do it?" asked Golan Tervize.
a) Isaac Asimov, *Foundation and Earth*, 1986
b) Larry Niven, *The Integral Trees*, 1983
c) Terry Prachett, *The Colour of Magic*, 1983

38. The sun was low in the west when the herd reached Remuda, Arizona, which is probably too small to be called a town.
a) Gene Tuttle, *Enough Rope to Hang*, 1985
b) Lia Matera, *Where Lawyers Fear to Tread*, 1987
c) Marcia Muller, *Wolf in the Shadows*, 1993

39. He looked down, confusedly wondering where he was as a person does when he awakens in a strange place.
a) Don Coldsmith, *The Flower in the Mountain*, 1988
b) Bud Vanzant, *Five Coffins for Hadleyville*, 1989
c) Randy Wayne White, *The Heat Islands*, 1992

40. The old woman—80 if she's a day—distorts perspective, throws off scale.
a) Susan Dodd, *Mamaw*, 1988
b) Leo P. Kelley, *Luke Sutton: Hired Gun*, 1987
c) Howard Pelham, *Mountain Ambush*, 1988

41. Liam Cauliffe was waiting on the steps of the clapboard Presbyterian church when Jason Russell finally rode into Charity on a grey afternoon in October.
a) Chelsea Quinn Yarbro, *The Law in Charity*, 1989
b) Jean M. Auel, *The Mammoth Hunters*, 1985
c) Marcy Heidish, *The Torching*, 1992

42. As I grew out of childhood it began to dawn on me that there was something rather mysterious about my presence in the Silk House.
a) Victoria Holt, *Silk Vendetta*, 1987
b) Alison Harding, *Also Georgiana*, 1986
c) Lillian O'Donnell, *Falling Star*, 1979

43. "It might be useful," said the rich, womanly voice, "to model me as your guardian angel."
a) Andrew M. Greeley, *Angel Fire*, 1988
b) Dean Koontz, *Strangers*, 1986
c) James Lee Burck, *Dixie City Jam*, 1994

44. For three weeks the young killer actually lived in the walls of an extraordinary 15-room beach house.
a) James Patterson, *Kiss the Girls*, 1995
b) Carl Hiaasen, *Tourist Season*, 1986
c) John Grisham, *The Chamber*, 1994

45. Her knuckles stood out white against the tan of her clenched hands.
a) Susan Dunlap, *Rogue Wave*, 1991
b) Beth Gutcheon, *Domestic Pleasures*, 1991
c) Norma Harris, *Trumpets of Silver*, 1991

46. The map under glass made no sense.
a) Nicholas Jose, *Avenue of Eternal Peace*, 1991
b) Andrew Coburn, *The Babysitter*, 1979
c) William Bayer, *Wallflower*, 1991

47. I had seldom felt so drained, so exhausted, both emotionally and physically.
a) Phyllis A. Whitney, *The Singing Stones*, 1990
b) Judith Guest and Rebecca Hill, *Killing Time in St. Cloud*, 1988
c) Virginia Anderson, *Storm Front*, 1992

48. I'd like to tell you about the time I was on the Short List—the short list to be the Democratic nominee for Vice President of the United States.
a) Jim Lehrer, *Short List*, 1992
b) John Ed Bradley, *Love and Obits*, 1992
c) John Banville, *Ghosts*, 1993

49. It was going to be a lousy day.
a) Andrew Klavan, *The Animal Hour*, 1993
b) Carol Brennan, *In the Dark*, 1994
c) Nancy Taylor Rosenberg, *Interest of Justice*, 1993

50. For more than two hundred years, the Owens women have been blamed for everything that has gone wrong in town.
a) Alice Hoffman, *Practical Magic*, 1995
b) Caroline Leavitt, *Living Other Lives*, 1995
c) Elizabeth Buchan, *Consider the Lily*, 1993

51. The bureaucrat fell from the sky.
a) Michael Svanwick, *Stations of the Tide*, 1991
b) Stephen R. Donaldson, *Forbidden Knowledge*, 1991
c) Robert Jordan, *The Dragon Reborn*, 1991

52. I never knew my mother.
a) Sheri S. Tepper, *Beauty*, 1991
b) Joe Haldeman, *The Hemingway Hoax*, 1990
c) William O. Turner, *Thief Hunt*, 1973

53. The Emperor of the Hundred Worlds stood at the head of the conference chamber, tall, gray, grim-faced.
a) Ben Bova & A.J. Austin, *To Save the Sun*, 1992
b) Stephen R. Donaldson, *A Dark and Hungry God Arises*, 1992
c) James P. Hogan, *The Multiplex Man*, 1992

54. Iconia was dead.
a) Carmen Carter, *Star Trek the Next Generation: The Devil's Heart*, 1993
b) Martin Caidin, *Indiana Jones and the Sky Pirates*, 1993
c) Dave Duncan, *Upland Outlaws*, 1993

55. The child looked up at the adult eagerly, wonderingly in that way that children had.
a) Peter David, *Star Trek the Next Generation: Q-Squared*, 1994
b) Charles Sheffield, *Godspeed*, 1993
c) R.F. Delderfield, *Mr. Sermon*, 1963

56. What is there to say of Arthur after all these years?
a) Stephen R. Lawhead, *Pendragon*, 1994
b) Sean Stuart, *Passion Play*, 1993
c) Herbert Lieberman, *Sandman, Sleep*, 1993

57. This time death was like being in the center of a whirlpool, inside the heart of a roaring tornado.
a) Ben Bova, *Orion Among the Stars*, 1995
b) Nancy Kress, *Beggars and Choosers*, 1994
c) William Shatner, *Tek Power*, 1994

58. He could hear the hounds coming on and now and then one of the archambos let out a wild yell, but he was afoot and all he could do was try to get above them.
a) John Reese, *Black-Snake Man*, 1976
b) Lee McElroy, *Long Way to Texas*, 1976
c) Fred Grove, *Warrior Road*, 1974

59. Old Wah Chee, the laundry man, was the best informed man in Deadwood, Dakota Territory.
a) Robert J. Steelman, *Portrait of a Sioux*, 1976
b) Amelia Barr, *Remember the Alamo*, 1979
c) Jay Shane, *They Called Him a Fox with Six-Guns*, 1971

60. Anyone who has ever dealt with the common cow will readily swear that the beast by far surpasses all other four-legged animals and most two-legged in the race for the title of the most miserable critter the Good Lord ever created.
a) Kent Conwell, *Panhandle Gold*, 1991
b) James A. Ratchie, *Over on the Lonesome Side*, 1991
c) John S. McCord, *Wyoming Giant*, 1992

61. Estcarp, the last-held land of the Old Ones in the latter days, was ruled by the Witch Women with the Power that had once been the heritage of all those from whom they had sprung.
a) Andre Norton, *Ware Hawk*, 1983
b) Harry Harrison, *A Stainless Steel Rat is Born*, 1985
c) Robert Silverberg, *Tom O'Bedlam*, 1985

62. Christy was an animal.
a) Pat Booth, *Miami*, 1991
b) Roseanne Bittner, *Thunder on the Plain*, 1992
c) Jennifer Blake, *Wildest Dreams*, 1992

63. "I need..."
a) Dean Koontz, *Mr. Murder*, 1993
b) Raymond Chandler, *The Simple Art of Murder*, 1950
c) Carter Travis Young, *Red Grass*, 1976

64. The coldsleep self was dreamless.
a) Vernor Vinge, *A Fire Upon the Deep*, 1992
b) L. Ron Hubbard, *Villainy Victorious*, 1987
c) Ray Bradbury, *Green Shadows*, 1992

65. Now it was early afternoon; an old lady's time for sleeping and bright dreams.
a) Pamela Frankau, *Over the Mountains*, 1967
b) Elizabeth Seifert, *Doctor with a Mission*, 1967
c) Piers Anthony, *Patham Mound*, 1991

66. The sky above the port was the color of television, tuned to a dead channel.
a) William Gibson, *Neuromancer*, 1984
b) C.J. Cherryh, *Chernevog*, 1990
c) Diana Wynne Jones, *A Sudden Wild Magic*, 1992

67. "I should feel sorrier," Raymond Horgan says.
a) Scott Turow, *Presumed Innocent*, 1987
b) James Patterson, *The Midnight Club*, 1989
c) Susan Howatch, *Scandalous Risks*, 1990

WHO SAID THAT? answers

1-a;   2-c;   8-a;
9-b;   10-   16-a;
17-b; 18- The answers to all quiz questions = A.

21-b; 22-a; 23-b; 24-c; 25-c; 26-b; 27-a; 28-a;
29-c; 30-c; 31-a; 32-b; 33-a; 34-a; 35-c; 36-b;
37-b; 38-b; 39-b; 40-a   41-c; 42-c; 43-a; 44-b;

45-a; 46-c; 47-a; 48-b; 49-b; 50-c; 51-a; 52-b;
53-c; 54-c; 55-a; 56-c; 57-b; 58-b; 59-a; 60-a;
61-c; 62-b; 63-a; 64-b; 65-b; 66-c; 67-a

Answers to page 6's
Pseudonym Quiz: Mystery Authors

1-a   2-l   3-k   4-d   5-h   6-p   7-j   8-s
9-m   10-e   11-w   12-t   13-v&x 14-g   15-q   16-r
17-c   18-u   19-u   19-f   20-f   21-i   22-b   23-o
24-f   25-x   26-z

Answers to page 9's
Pseudonym Quiz: Collaborative Teams

1-g   2-a   3-e   4-b   5-h   6-i   7-d   8-i
9-c   10-f

Answers to page 10's
Pseudonym Quiz: Mystery and Western Authors

1-i	2-e	3-g	4-c	5-c	6-f	7-d	8-i
9-a	10-b	11-i	12-b	13-e	14-e	15-i	16-c
17-f	18-e	19-f	20-e	21-i	22-d	23-h	24-j
25-k	26-j						

Answers to page 41's
Pseudonym Quiz: Science Fiction Authors

1-a	2-a	3-k	4-j	5-c	6-h	7-h	8-a
9-i	10-h	11-h	12-e	13-g	14-b	15-c	16-c
17-f	18-k	19-h	20-d	21-a	22-c	23-k	24-l
25-n	26-m						

Answers to page 44's
Pseudonym Quiz: Mainstream Authors

1-b   2-e   3-a   4-f   5-c   6-d

Answers to page 63's
Pseudonym Quiz: Romance Authors

1-b   2-a   3-c   4-b   5-d   6-e   7-b

About the Editor

Sharon Rendell-Smock began her writing career at age nineteen as a Florida newspaper features writer.

A graduate of the University of Illinois, she had nearly achieved a master's degree in social work when she decided to pursue her main interest—writing.

She went on to write more than 20 computer software user manuals.

In 1995, her book, *Living with Big Cats: The Story of Jungle Larry, Safari Jane, and David Tetzlaff*, earned a national award for nonfiction writing.

Rendell-Smock lives in southwest Florida where she performs freelance writing, editing, and proofreading, and is working on her next book.

Books by

Sharon Rendell-Smock

* *Getting Hooked: Fiction's Opening Sentences 1950s-1990s* $7.95 (U.S.)
(I.S.B.N. 0-9654981-0-7)

* **The award-winning book**
Living with Big Cats: The Story of Jungle Larry, Safari Jane, and David Tetzlaff

(includes over 100 black & white, and color photographs of tigers, leopards, lions, trainers) $11.95 (U.S.)
(I.S.B.N. 0-9642604-0-9)

Shipping $3.00 regardless of quantity ordered

Order from:

1-800-356-9315

Toll free   Credit Card Orders Welcome

Upper Access, Inc.
P.O. Box 457
Hinesburg VT 05461